FERNS

WILD THINGS MAKE A COMEBACK IN THE GARDEN

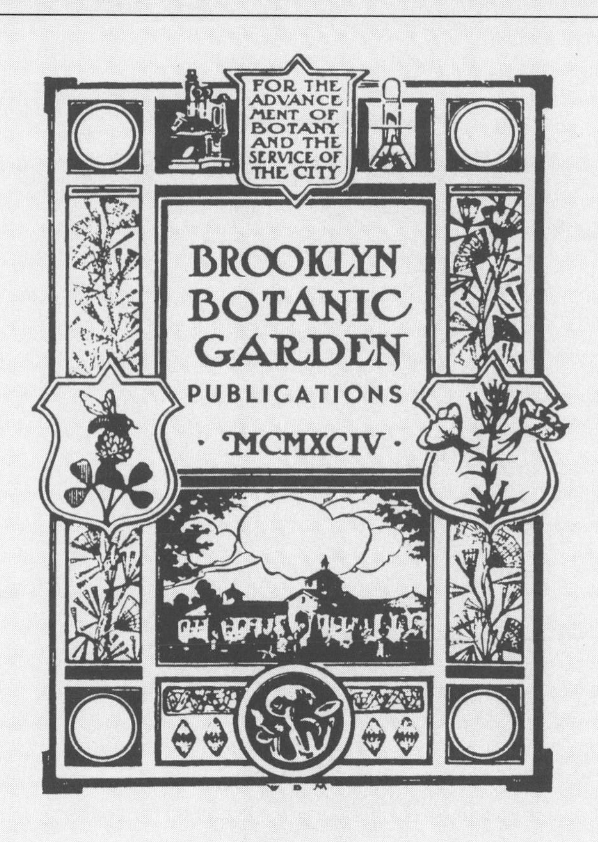
FOR THE ADVANCEMENT OF BOTANY AND THE SERVICE OF THE CITY
BROOKLYN BOTANIC GARDEN
PUBLICATIONS
· MCMXCIV ·

FERNS 

WILD THINGS MAKE A COMEBACK IN THE GARDEN

C. Colston Burrell ✓ Guest Editor

BBG gardening guides are published quarterly at 1000 Washington Ave., Brooklyn, NY 11225

Subscription included in Brooklyn Botanic Garden membership dues ($25.00 per year)

ISSN 0362-5850 ISBN # 0-945352-82-4

Contributors

C. Colston Burrell is a garden designer, writer, photographer and lifelong fernophile. He is President of Native Landscape Design and Restoration, Ltd. of Minneapolis, a design firm specializing in the creation of environmentally appropriate gardens. He has grown over 60 varieties of hardy ferns in Virginia and Minnesota.

Judith Jones is a self-taught fern specialist. Her nursery, Fancy Fronds, in Seattle, has introduced six new ferns to the American nursery trade. She has lectured throughout North America and England and her nursery's displays of hardy ferns have won four gold medals at flower shows tin the Northwest. She is a self-proclaimed pteridomaniac.

Charlotte A. Jones-Roe is the Assistant Director for Conservation and Development at the North Carolina Botanical Garden in Chapel Hill, North Carolina. She has conducted field studies, writes about gardening with native ferns and offers classes on identification and culture of the ferns of the Southeast.

Nancy Swell grows and propagates a wide variety of hardy ferns in her garden in Richmond, Virginia. She is an active member of The American Fern Society, The British Pteridological Society and The Hardy Fern Foundation and is a self-proclaimed fern fernatic.

Table of Contents

INTRODUCTION

BY C. COLSTON BURRELL

ELCOME TO the world of ferns. You're about to become enchanted by one of the oldest groups of plants on earth. These "primitive" plants have colonized most terrestrial and aquatic habitats throughout the world. Although the diversity of fern species is highest in the tropics, hardy temperate ferns suitable for our gardens are found throughout North America, Europe, Asia and India, as well as temperate regions of the Southern Hemisphere. In fact, many species are cosmopolitan — that is, they are found on all the continents, proof of their ancient origin.

Ferns impart a calm grace to gardens that no other group of plants offers. They beguile us with just their leaves. The first fiddleheads of spring unfurl a world of green as diverse and intricate as any meticulously orchestrated border scheme. No gaudy display of flowers is necessary. From the filigreed lace of the lady fern to the bold, erect swords of deer fern, fronds provide form, color and texture to suit the most stringent design criteria.

Ferns are never static. As the fiddleheads unroll and the blades expand, their color darkens from pale lime green to rich green, passing through all the shades in between. Some ferns have fronds tinged with

Left and right: *Athyrium niponicum* 'Pictum', Japanese painted fern red, while others sport silver-gray blades with rosy-pink stipes. By late summer, the fronds may turn soft yellow, tawny brown or blazing russet. Even the shriveled brown fronds enliven the winter landscape. Evergreen species provide year-round verdure. Whoever said ferns were boring must have been blinded by a dahlia as big as a dinner plate.

Despite their apparent delicacy, ferns thrive under conditions that few other plants tolerate. They are tough, durable and adaptable. Best of all, they are beautiful. The ground-dwelling ferns are popular, easy-care garden plants. They grow wild in open woodlands, swamps, marshes and bogs and deep in conifer forests. They grow on shaded banks, along streams, on decaying logs or atop mossy hummocks. Most are readily available from nurseries. Rock-dwelling ferns inhabit bare cliff faces, shaded overhangs and the sides of pounding waterfalls. Some species scramble through the thin humus on boulders and in the rubble of talus slopes. Many of the choicest rock ferns are best left to experts, although a few are good performers. A few of the best rock ferns are included in the encyclopedia section of this book.

A unique set of terminology is used to describe ferns. In order to understand the text and the encyclopedia entries, you must master a few new terms. They are not difficult; they are just new. Refer to the glossary in the back of the book for the definitions you need.

In the pages that follow, you will find an in-depth exploration of fern structure, and an easy-to-understand explanation of the fern life cycle, which baffled scientists for centuries. You're guided, step by step, through the collection, preparation, sowing and germination of spores, as well as the transplanting and hardening-off of young plants. Judith Jones, the author of these chapters and a professional grower of ferns, also discusses the various fast, easy, asexual propagation techniques more familiar to gardeners, such as division. Veteran fern grower Nancy Swell draws on her years of experience to provide clear, no-nonsense advice on the planting and care of ferns. She makes it so simple that even the most reticent gardeners will be ready to inaugurate their first fern garden.

The encyclopedia of ferns presents descriptions and cultural requirements of more than 65 easy-to-grow, hardy species. In this section, I have provided suggestions for garden compositions and companions for each entry. Many outstanding cultivars are mentioned as well. Hardiness zones are provided as a guide but are by no means conclusive. Many of the non-native ferns are fairly new to mainstream horticulture and have not been grown in the colder zones. Try them out. Don't be afraid to experiment. Many of these plants may prove hardy well beyond their known range. To better serve gardeners on a regional level, I assembled lists of the ten best ferns for the major regions of North America where favorable climate and ample rainfall make fern cultivation feasible and environmentally appropriate. In areas with insufficient precipitation to support any but the most specialized rock-dwelling ferns, I do not recommend fern cultivation. In areas such as the Desert Southwest, the water needed to support a

Below: ***Cystopteris bulbifera*****, bulblet bladder fern, native to eastern and central North America**

lush fern garden is best left flowing down the Colorado River.

Charlotte Jones-Roe has assembled a list of some of the continent's most outstanding fern collections, where you can go for first-hand information and inspiration. Her list is based on the American Association of Botanic Gardens and Arboreta's Plant Collections Directory. Any omissions are unintentional. If we have missed an important collection, please let us know and we will list it in subsequent editions of this handbook.

Sources of nursery-propagated ferns are provided so you know where to acquire ferns that have been propagated by growers, not collected in the wild, and therefore do not threaten wild populations or habitats. The list of fern societies will connect you with others who share a fascination with this intriguing group of plants.

Thanks to the contributors for sharing their expertise. Thanks also to Pamela Harper, Judith Jones, Galen Gates, Roger Hammer, Joanne Pavia, Jerry Pavia and Sue Olsen for their superb photographs. I'm also grateful to the following people for help in compiling the regional lists of recommended species:

Logan Calhoun, Kings Creek Landscaping, Dallas, Texas
Bob Hyland, Strybing Arboretum, San Francisco, California
Panayoti Kelaidis, Denver Botanic Gardens, Denver, Colorado
Cheryl Lowe, Garden in the Woods, Framingham, Massachusetts
David Price, Bok Tower Gardens, Lake Wales, Florida

I hope this handbook offers new insights and provides fresh inspiration for veteran fern fanciers. For those of you who are neophytes, prepare to discover an ever-widening circle of fronds. Let's hope your garden can accommodate the crowd.

WHAT MAKES A FERN A FERN

BY JUDITH I. JONES

OST GARDENERS think of ferns as plants with finely divided "feathery" foliage and no flowers. They also describe the foliage of some flowering plants that are not ferns as "ferny." So what key characteristics distinguish true ferns from plants with fern-like foliage? The absence of flowers, fruits and seeds is certainly the most obvious feature. When examined at the appropriate time of the year mature ferns generally have rusty patches on the underside of the foliage. These are the structures that produce spores, the unicellular structures involved in fern reproduction. Linnaeus classified ferns into genera based on the position and shape of these spore-producing organs.

The number of temperate fern genera is not too daunting; only 15 percent of the world's fern species occur in the temperate zone. A very small fraction of these are available to gardeners. To simplify matters even more, the most popular and easily grown species come from a small number of genera. And only a few species have yielded many of the cultivars that gardeners grow (a cultivar is a plant specially selected or bred for horticultural use). Becoming familiar with the ferns native to your area will give you a good foundation for learning about other species.

FERN STRUCTURE

To be competent at fern identification you don't need a laboratory full of equipment. All you need are a good 10X to 20X hand lens, a few good fern identification guides and, if possible, some help from a local expert or enthusiast. You don't even need the hand lens to see most of the important fern parts.

Although mature ferns consist of roots, stems and leaves, just as other, more familiar plants do, different terms are used to describe the various fern parts.

CROZIERS One very distinctive feature common to most ferns is the manner in which the newly emerging foliage unfolds in a scroll-like fashion. The newly developing fern leaves are called croziers or fiddleheads. The form of the crozier — ranging from a tightly coiled geometric spiral to a lax shepherd's crook — and the way it gradually expands is often a clue to the identity of the fern. Some ferns that don't exhibit these coiled croziers are the moonworts, staghorn ferns and grape ferns.

FROND ELEMENTS The most obvious part of any fern is the portion above ground, which is known as the frond. The frond is further delineated into the stipe and the blade or lamina. The stipe is the stem-like portion of the frond that bears no foliage and connects the leafy blade to the mostly underground rhizome. The blade comprises the supporting stalk — or rachis, if compound, and the

Left: Croziers of the western sword fern, *Polystichum munitum*

attached primary leafy segments or pinnae. Pinnae (plural of pinna) may be divided into one or more distinct secondary segments known collectively as pinnules.

Rhizome and fronds are often clothed with a protective covering (indument) of hairs and/or scales. Hairs are only one cell wide and one or more cells long. Scales, which are several cells wide and long but mostly one cell thick, are broader. The absence or presence of hairs and/or scales, especially their overall shape and color, are other clues to the identification of ferns.

Another characteristic used to classify ferns is the veins. Veins run from margin to midvein. Where these branch but do not form a united network of veins, they are referred to as free. While most ferns have free veins, some do have veins that unite and form distinctive networks helpful in identification.

FROND DISSECTION The overall shape of the blade, the characteristic outline of its margins and the number of segments into which it is divided all help distinguish one fern from another.

Special terms are used to describe the degree of frond dissection: Undissected blades are called simple. A blade that is divided once, completely to the rachis, with each pinna narrowed at the base or stalked where it meets the main rachis is pinnate. Bipinnate blades have two divisions, the pinna, which is attached to the main rachis, and the pinnules, which are attached to the pinna rachis, also called the costa. Tripinnate and quadripinnate are further degrees of dissection. To determine the degree of dissection or "pinnateness," start counting from the largest division, the pinna, and continue counting each complete division after that. Another way is to follow the stipe to the rachis at the base of the first pinnae and count the rachis as zero. Then count the number of branches off the rachis. For example, a bipinnate fern has two branches off the rachis: the pinna is one and the pinnule is two, so the frond is bipinnate.

There is another kind of dissection to consider — partial dissection of a pinna or pinnule. This trait of not being divided all the way to a narrow attachment to the main rachis or pinna rachis is termed pinnatifid. Thus, pinnate-pinnatifid means that the blade is divided more than one time but not quite into two distinct divisions. Blades may also be more divided at the base and less divided at the top.

This isn't as complicated as it sounds. Look closely at a few ferns from your garden. A little practice will make the botanical lingo much less baffling.

RHIZOMES An understanding of the structure and function of the rhizome is crucial to growing ferns successfully. Rhizomes are also key to the vegetative propagation of ferns. However inconspicuous the rhizome may be, it not only provides a vital link between the roots and the frond, but also determines the plant's habit. The rhizome may be erect, holding the fronds in a close, vase-like cluster, or it may recline or creep horizontally, with fronds arising in an irregular cluster fashion. The symme-

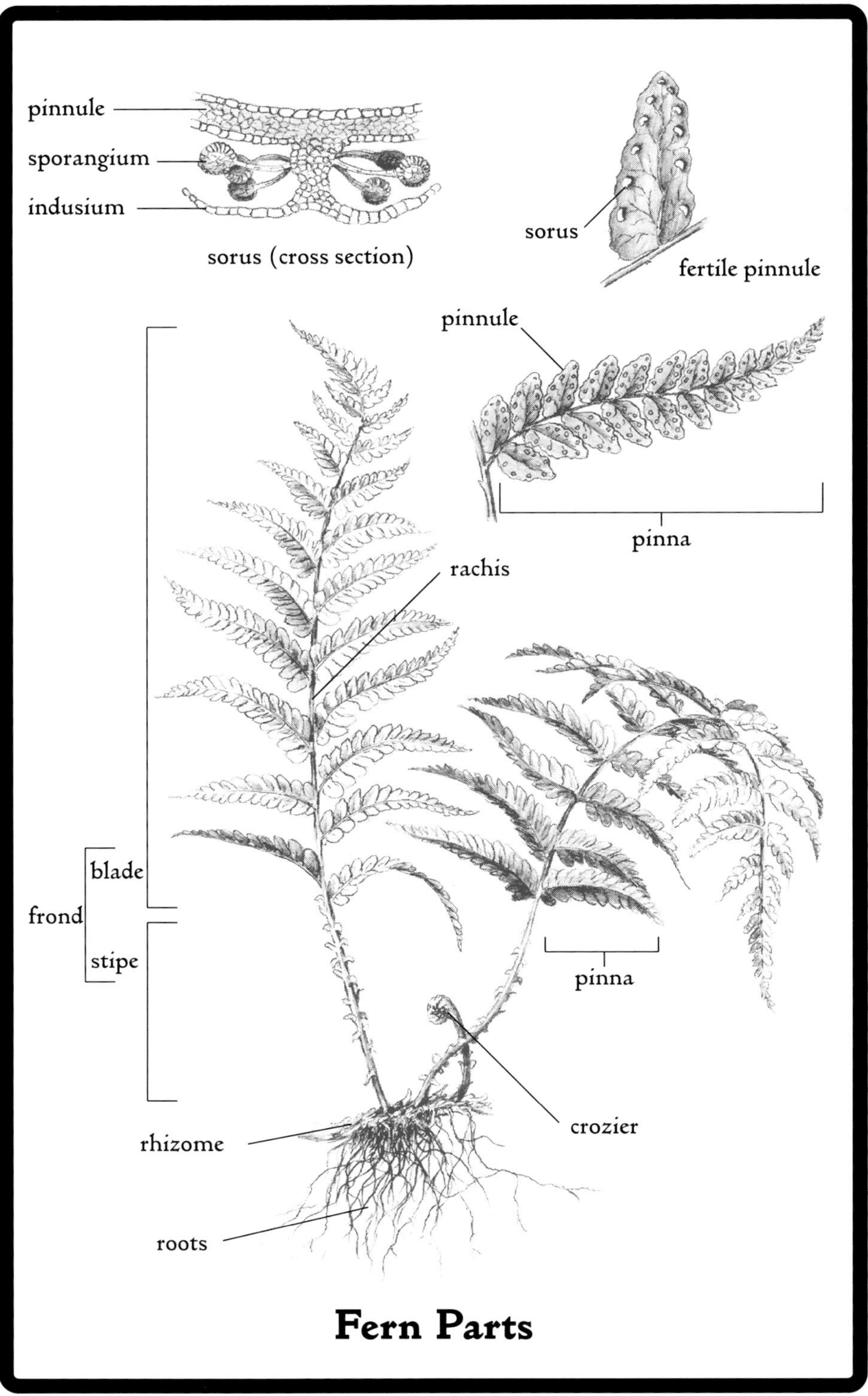

Fern Parts

STEVE BUCHANAN

try of the fronds arising from upright rhizomes is certainly a major factor in our visual appreciation of ferns that display this habit. An erect rhizome gives rise to a crown.

Reclining rhizomes look like upright rhizomes that have toppled over. Some, such as *Dryopteris stewartii,* produce croziers arranged in a curious spiral-like curve, but are similiar in appearance to their erect counterparts when their fronds are fully flushed. Horizontally creeping rhizomes may be closely or loosely branched, affecting the manner in which their fronds arise. Long-established plants may appear somewhat different in habit because their extensive colonies of overlapping rhizomes produce a denser foliage arrangement.

Fern roots can help in the identification of a species. For example, the roots of *Osmunda regalis,* the royal fern, are spongy, overlapping mats. Healthy roots are a lovely, translucent caramel color with creamy yellow growing tips. Older roots are dark brown or black but still have creamy yellow root tips.

FERTILE FRONDS The first fronds produced in spring are sterile fronds. The fertile fronds, those bearing sporangia, the spore-producing organs, arise later in the season. Fertile fronds may be the same shape as sterile fronds. On some species they may be a slightly modified version of the sterile frond or even a completely different shape and structure altogether. For example, the sterile and fertile fronds of *Athyrium filix-femina* are similar. Those of *Osmunda claytoniana* are slightly different, and those of *Matteuccia struthiopteris* are entirely different. When a fern exhibits this condition of distinctly different sterile and fertile fronds it is called dimorphic. Observing whether the sterile and fertile fronds are identical or different is another tool in the identification of ferns.

SPORE-PRODUCING ORGANS Remember that the system of classification upon which fern identification is based revolves around their spore-producing organs. Individual clusters of sporangia are referred to as sori, in the singular sorus, and they may be grouped in round, oblong, linear or other configurations. The sori may be scattered along the veins or vein endings or cover the entire underside of the frond. Some sori may be enveloped by a special tissue-thin mantle known as the indusium (in the plural, indusia). Marginal sori are frequently overlapped by a flap of folded blade tissue which is called a false indusium. The shape and arrangement of the sori as well as the shape and presence of the indusia or false indusia are of key importance in fern identification.

THE LIFE CYCLE OF FERNS

Because ferns lack flowers, their reproductive cycle was long shrouded in mystery. It wasn't until the 17th century that botanists came to realize that spores give rise to more ferns. In the mid-19th century when the microscope was

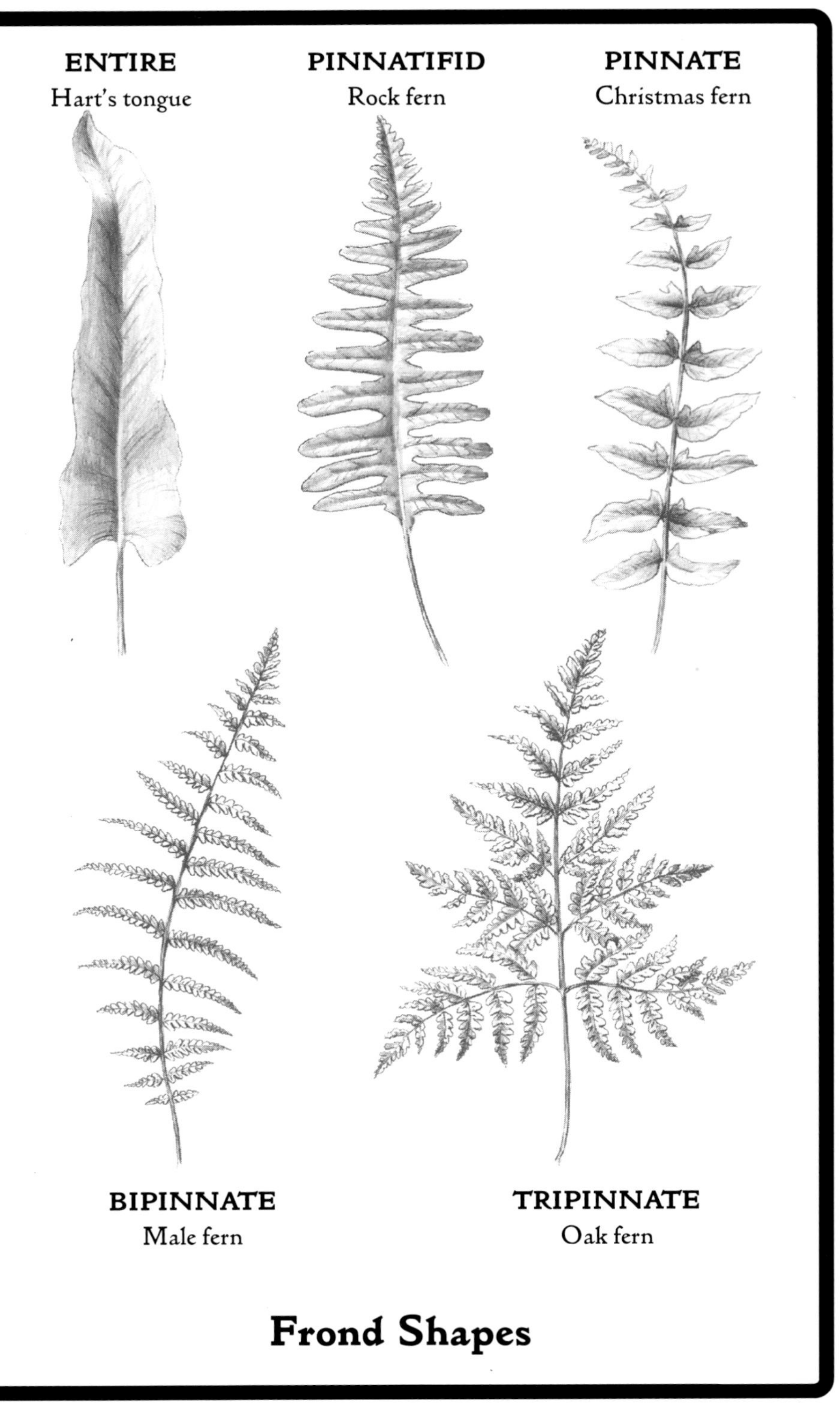

STEVE BUCHANAN

refined, spore germination finally could be studied scientifically.

ALTERNATING GENERATIONS A two-phase reproductive cycle known as the alternation of generations is characteristic of ferns. The conspicuous phase that we recognize as a fern and in which spores are produced is known as the sporophyte generation. The sexual phase, a tiny plant by comparison, is called the gametophyte. To understand this complex life history, let's begin with the formation of spores within the sporangia of the sporophyte generation.

SPORES Most ferns produce 64 spores within each sporangium. In the center of the developing sporangium there is a single cell that divides to produce all the spores. It divides into identical cells, a process known as mitosis. These cells continue to divide until there are 16 cells, called spore mother cells. Now each spore mother cell undergoes a special kind of nuclear division known as meiosis, during which one cell produces four cells, each with only half the number of chromosomes (thus, if the mother cell contains 14, each daughter cell will contain only seven). Not only is the chromosome number reduced, but there is also interchange of genetic material between chromosomes. Thus the four new cells, destined in ferns to become spores, will be genetically different from each other and from the original mother cell. Set free from the sporophyte each spore, given the right environmental conditions, will grow by mitosis into a gametophyte (prothallus). It will produce eggs and/or sperm cells (see below). Fusion of these in pairs produces zygotes, each having the original chromosome number (say 14, using the example above) and the capability of growing into a sporophyte (see the illustration on the opposite page). Some ferns undergo more mitotic divisions before meiosis.

PROTHALLUS A spore released from a parent plant that lands on moist soil begins to divide. As the cell divides it gradually forms a spongy, roughly heart-shaped cushion of cells. Visible to the naked eye, this is the gametophyte plant or prothallus (the plural is prothalli), on which the sexual organs involved in fertilization emerge. Like the more conspicuous spore-producing plant, the prothallus has root-like hairs, called rhizoids, that absorb and conduct nutrients and water to the cells.

While the edges of this "cushion" may be only one cell thick, the center is several cells thick and it is here that the sexual organs are generally found. Although prothalli may be bisexual, they are usually either male or female. The female egg-producing organs, archegonia, (the singular is archegonium) occur near the notch of the heart-shaped prothallus. The male sperm-producing organs, antheridia, (the singular is antheridium) occur on the "wings" and opposite the notch of the prothallus. Each archegonium has a chimney-like protuberance that is flared at the top to receive the sperm, which fertilizes the egg at the

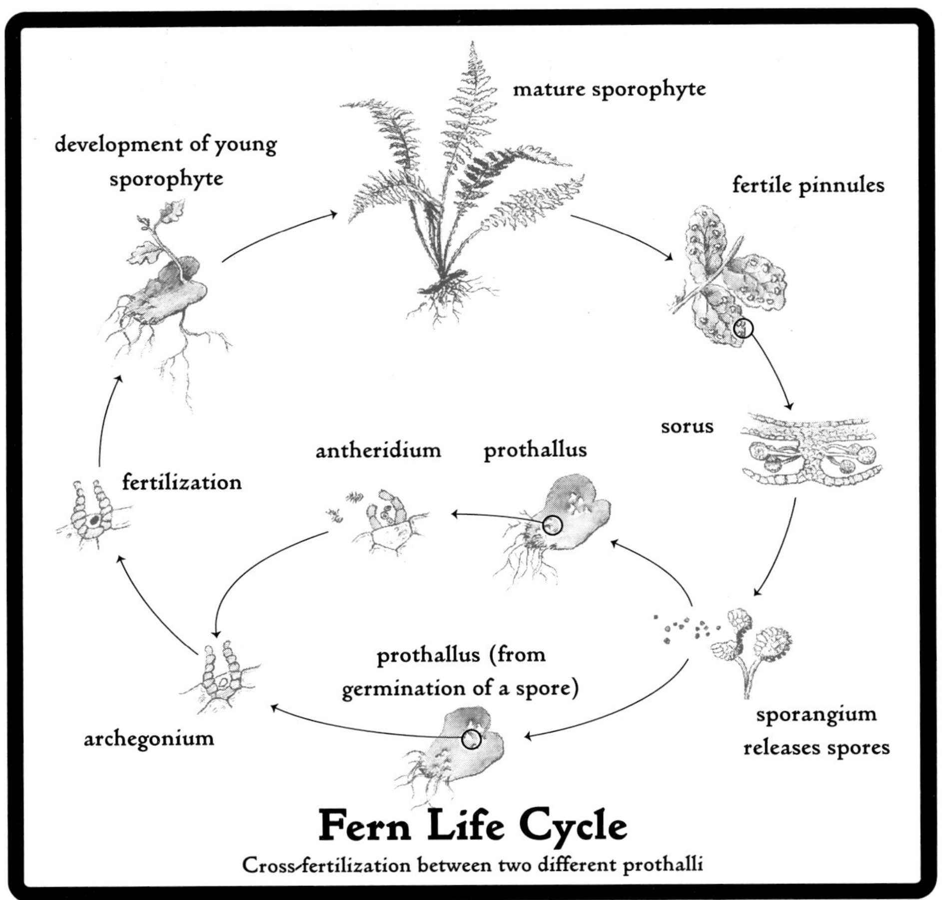

STEVE BUCHANAN

base. Each antheridium is a minute, capsule-like sac where the sperm grow.

The life cycle diagram above illustrates the current understanding of the reproductive process known as out-crossing — that is, fertilization between two different gametophytes (as opposed to self-crossing or self-fertilization). Although each prothallus may be capable of fertilizing itself, experiments have shown that the resulting sporophytes are inbred and often fail to thrive. Cross-fertilization helps ensure genetic diversity.

When an egg is fertilized by a spermatozoid the chromosome number doubles, returning to what it was in the parent sporophyte. The fertilized egg, or zygote, begins to divide to form the young sporophyte. Initially, a short-lived primary root grows. It is supplanted by roots growing from the newly forming rhizome. With a food- and water-absorbing system in place, the first fronds emerge. These bear only a remote resemblance to their mature parents, especially in the more dissected species. Successive fronds increasingly resemble those of the parent plants.

 GROWING FERNS FROM SPORES 

BY JUDITH I. JONES

IF YOU'VE STUMBLED a bit over the specialized terms used to describe ferns, the prospect of propagating them from spores may seem much too intimidating. But you don't have to be a botanist to be successful at propagating ferns from spores. As you become acquainted with the ferns in your garden and their biological cycles, these terms will become second nature, and growing your own ferns from spores will seem much less daunting.

SOURCES OF SPORES Acquiring some spores to sow is the first order of business. There are two ways to obtain spores. You can join international fern societies with spore exchanges, such as the American Fern Society or the British Pteridological Society. There are also many excellent regional societies that offer spores. Members of these organizations are able to order spores for a very modest fee per packet. The listing of spores available can be quite extensive, so this is an excellent way to try new ferns or find very unusual and rare ones. Keep in mind, however, that the particular type of spore that you request may not be in the packet that arrives in the mail, even if the label says it is. These spore exchanges depend on donations from their members, and mistakes are made. Sometimes stray spores of other ferns get mixed in the packet due to poorly cleansed fronds or contamination during packaging. Always reserve a healthy bit of skepticism about any spore-grown fern until you have verified its identity by looking it up or asking an experienced grower about it. What's more, spore-exchange packets may contain mostly sporangial debris mixed with hairs and scales from the frond, with very few spores. Sowing spores mixed with this much chaff generally leads to failure and frustration. On the other hand, when a fern is otherwise unobtainable, it may be worth risking failure on the off chance that a few spores will succeed.

If you already have a collection of ferns or have permission to gather fertile fronds from someone else's collection or from the wild, then you don't have to depend on spore exchanges. Gathering spores only requires patience, persistence and attention to detail. A 10X hand lens is useful for beginner spore collectors because it enables you to determine whether the sori are immature, mature or past mature.

Remember that each fern genus has a distinctive soral pattern with or without distinctive indusia (see "What Makes a Fern a Fern"). For example, ferns in the genus *Dryopteris* have round sori protected by kidney-shaped indusia. For the most part immature sori are a pale whitish color, although there are exceptions, such as *Dryopteris erythrosora,* which goes through a brilliant pinkish-red to ruby-red stage before maturing. The indusium closely envelops the sporangia, leaving only a slight span between its lower edge and the surface of the pinna. As the spores inside each sporangium mature they get darker, until they are a deep brown or black. The edges of the indusium begin to lift, allowing the ripe spores to bulge out. Eventually the indusium shrivels up, and the exposed spores are ready to be catapulted into the air.

Not all spores mature to a deep brown or black, nor are all sporangia covered with an indusium. Polypodiums are ripe when they are buttercup yellow, osmundas when they are green, and both have probably been dispersed, or dehisced, when the soral remains are a deep, burnished old gold. Although the sporangia of both these genera are without indusia, they have a similar dispersal mechanism to those that do.

THE SPORANGIA The sporangium in most ferns is a thin-walled case, usually on a stalk, that has a ring of thick-walled cells known as the annulus, which aids in opening the sporangium when the spores are fully mature. This belt-like ring of cells encircling the sporangium resembles a medieval knight's visor when viewed from the side. When the spores are ripe, the annulus breaks near the base of one side, tearing the sporangium apart, and arches backward. The annulus snaps forward abruptly, flinging the spores away from the frond. You can easily observe this phenomenon with a 20X hand lens by placing a ripe pinna or frond under a bright light. The heat from the light will dry the sori and trigger the annuli into action. This is a thrilling sight but be forewarned that you'll have thousands of spores all over yourself and the immediate vicinity!

COLLECTING SPORES This clever spore dispersal system works to your advantage as a spore collector. Fronds or pinnae with mature sporangia can be placed sporangia-side down on a sheet of clean paper onto which the spores will be released. If you have a large collection of different ferns growing together or your ferns grow among mosses you may want to first cleanse the fronds to cut down on foreign contaminants. Briefly soak or swish picked material in a 5 to 10 percent bleach solution, rinse with running water, shake and place the fronds, sporangia side down, on clean paper. Paper with a smooth finish is best for packaging spores. Because I harvest large quantities of spores from ferns of all sizes I use a large roll of white butcher paper from which I cut the sizes required. Each piece can be made into an origami-style envelope suitable for storing the spores until they are needed (see below). Write the name of the fern, if known, date collected, where collected and any other information you'd like to remember.

RIPE SPORES How do you know when to pick fronds or pinnae to harvest spores? In addition to the color of ripe spores, there are other conspicuous features to look for. The most telling sign that the sporangia have dehisced are frayed, scruffy-looking sori. Whereas ripe sori are plump and firm with little brown, black, yellow or green spheres, spent sori are generally a dull cinnamon brown. If

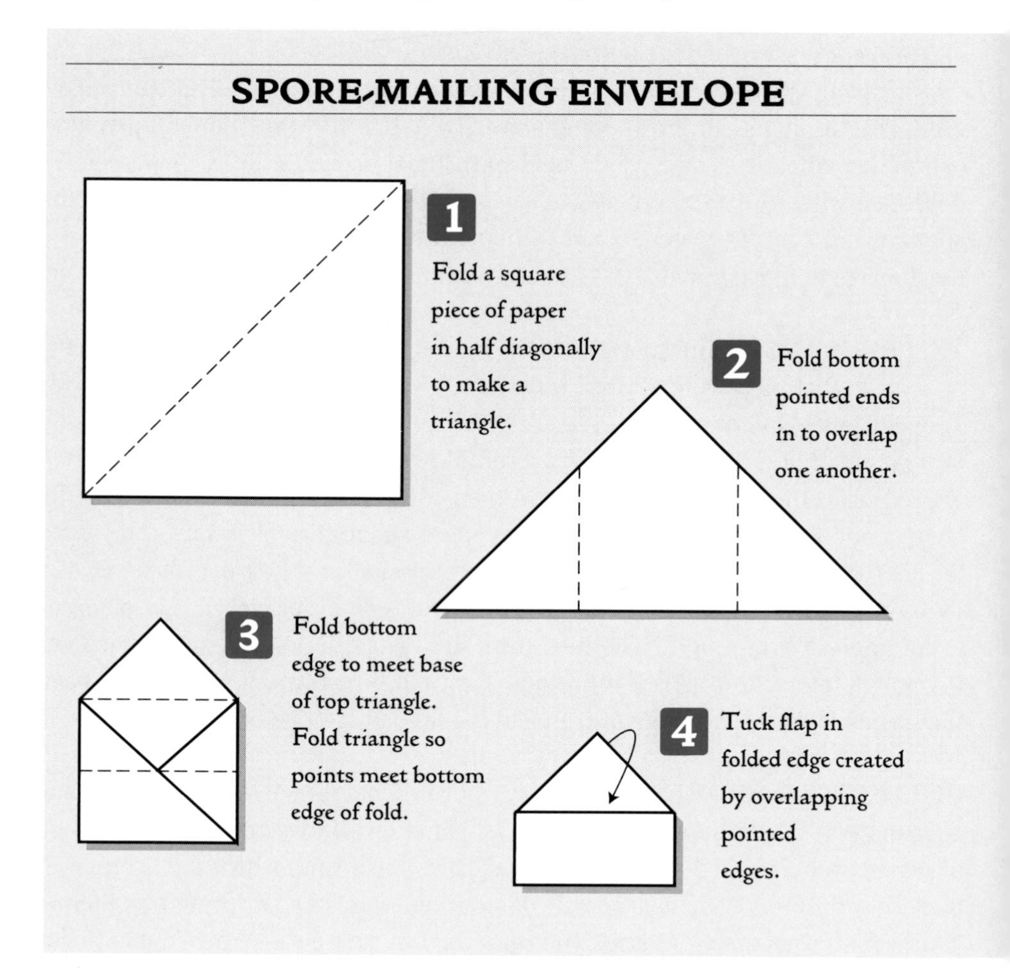

you still aren't sure when to pick the fronds, do a little experimenting. The sporangia mature from the base to the apex of the blades, and not all blades mature at the same time. Remove the pinnae or pinnules from different sections of one or more blades. Place these in separate packets carefully labeled so you will know which fragment yielded the most spores. Don't forget to closely observe each sample so that next time you'll be able to recognize the ripe spores.

CLEANING SPORES Cleanliness is the key to successful propagation from spores. After you've cleansed the fertile frond in the 5 to 10 percent bleach solution, tap the frond to release spores still stuck to it and discard it. The spores will be mixed with sporangial debris and maybe even some scales and hairs from the frond. The debris is lighter in color or at least a slightly different color from the spores and weighs less. By carefully lifting the paper and gently tapping from underneath, you can coax this fluffy debris to slide off the paper and discard it.

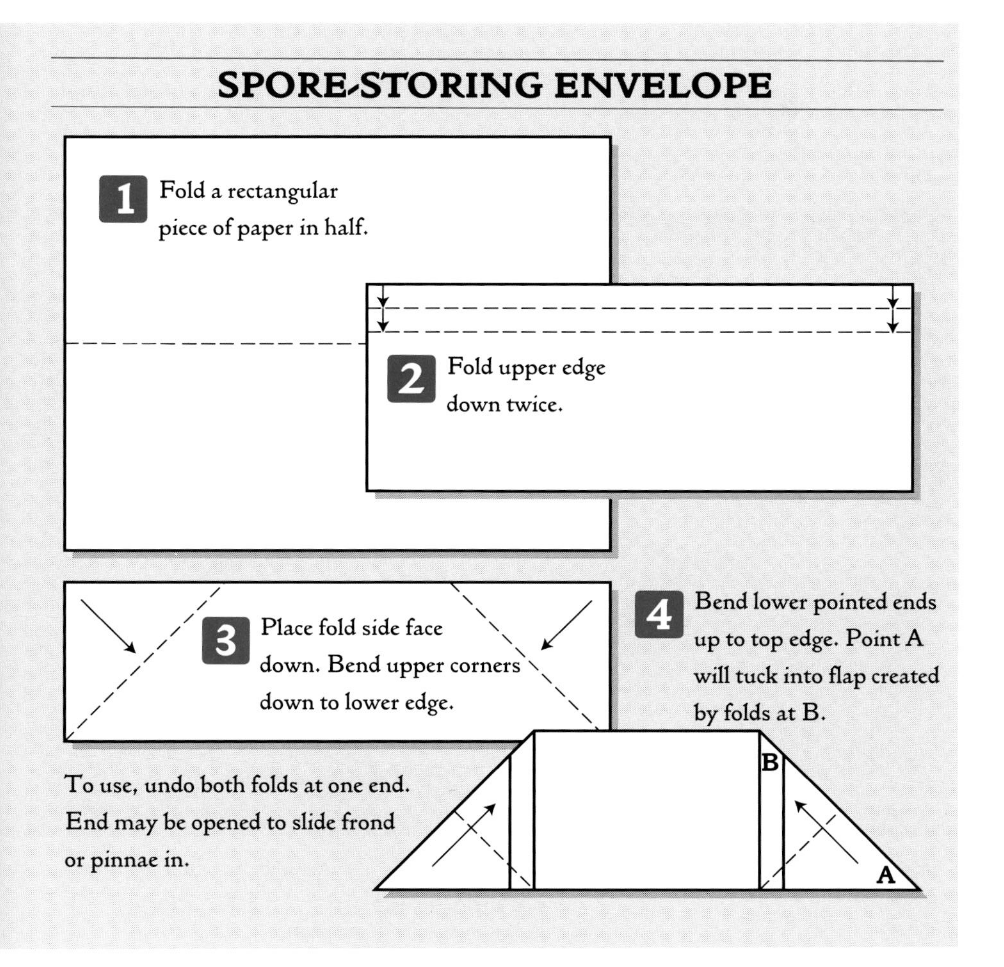

An even more thorough cleaning can be achieved by sifting the spores through tissue paper used for cleaning camera lenses. I use two pieces laid across one another with the grain facing in opposite directions. The spores, generally smaller and heavier than the unwanted debris, fall through, leaving the debris in the lens paper. You can also use a fine screen; however, thoroughly cleaning it between siftings is time-consuming.

Spores can be cleaned either well ahead of sowing or when you are ready to sow. I generally tap and remove fronds and do a preliminary "paper tap" cleaning before filing my spores away. I save the final operation of sifting through the lens-tissue for when I sow, as this tissue is a wonderful method for sprinkling spores evenly over the sterile medium.

MEDIUM AND CONTAINERS There are no hard and fast rules about what kind of medium or container is best. Use what is available and works best for you. One thing is crucial, however: both the medium and the container must be as sterile as possible.

Possible containers range from disposable plastic cups to nursery flats. A tight-fitting cover is essential to maintain humidity and keep out air-borne contaminants such as the spores of other ferns, fungi and mosses. Grocery stores

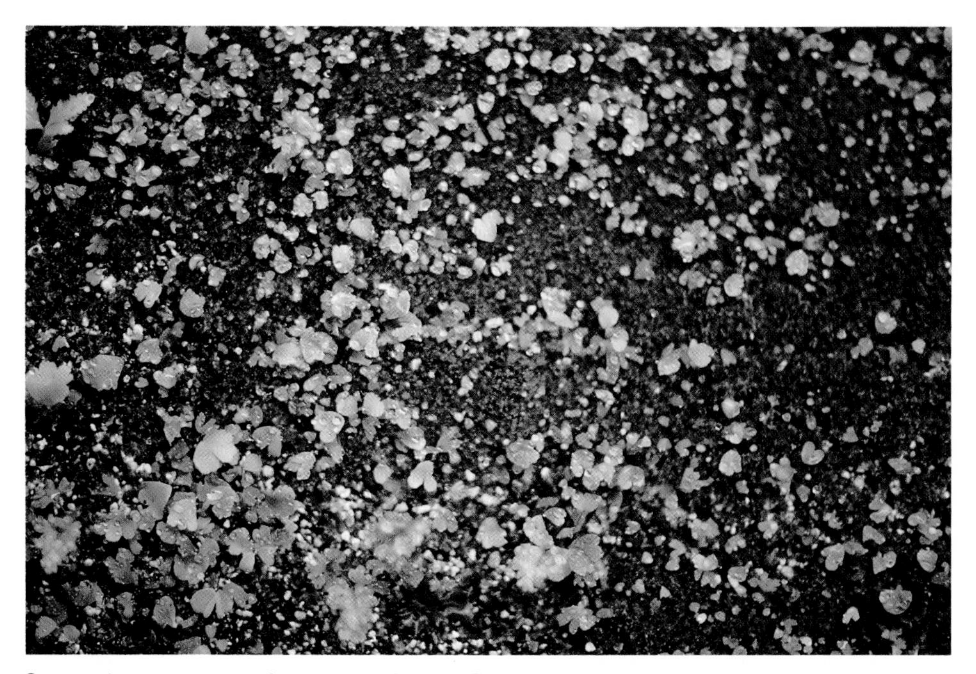

Sporophytes emerge from a solid mat of prothalli. The length of time required for the prothalli to produce young sporelings ranges from 6 to 12 months.

offer an array of containers with clear plastic lids. Plastic food wrap and rubber bands are an inexpensive way to cover almost any container. Some growers use vaseline to maintain a seal between the lid and the container. The container may or may not have drainage holes, depending on your set-up. Watering can be accomplished by misting from the top or by capillary action from the bottom. There are advantages and disadvantages to both. Every time you open the cover to mist, contaminants can enter. However, sometimes bottom watering must be supplemented with overhead misting to provide a film of water for fertilization.

The various media used to raise ferns from spores include garden soil, well rotted and sifted compost, milled sphagnum moss, peat moss, vermiculite, perlite and assorted combinations of these. The *Fern Growers Manual* by Barbara Joe Hoshizaki (Knopf, 1979) thoroughly covers the various possible combinations. Soilless mixes are used by most commercial growers because they can be purchased premixed or mixed to meet specific requirements and are easily sterilized. The mix I prefer is two parts perlite to one part peat moss with micronutrients and timed release fertilizer added (see box on page 27).

The quickest way to sterilize the growing mix is in the microwave. Wet the medium to a sloppy mud-pie consistency in a plastic bag. (Grocery bags with handles are excellent.) Place the bag in a microwaveable dish tall enough to

A flat of young crested scollies, *Asplenium scolopendrium* 'Cristatum'. Once ferns reach 15 to 25 percent of their mature size they can be divided into single plants.

catch the excess water that comes out of the bag during the steaming process. (Be sure to tuck the opening of the bag down into the dish or water may come oozing out the microwave door!) You may need to experiment to find out how long to "cook" the mix as microwaves vary. I set my ten-level microwave on level 3 and cook for 50 to 60 minutes. You can also sterilize mixes in a regular oven, baking for two hours at 250 to 300° F. Two large metal mixing bowls make a nice steam chamber but any large pot with a tight-fitting lid will do. The mix should reach a temperature of 180° F for 30 minutes. Use a meat thermometer pushed in to the center of the mix to determine the total amount of time needed.

Next, pack the sterilized mix into the sterilized containers. Containers should be rinsed in a 10 percent bleach solution; rinsing is optional. Putting containers through a complete dishwashing cycle should also sterilize them sufficiently. I prefer to tamp down the mix in the containers when it is still quite warm, as the warm air that rises up through it helps prevent foreign air-borne spores from drifting down to the sterile surface. If the containers have drainage holes, you can also sprinkle the surface of the mix with very hot water before covering the containers to prevent contamination. Containers without drainage holes should be covered and sprayed with sterile water just before sowing the spores, but not too much.

You don't have to sow spores to increase your collection of ferns. In some species, buds that grow on the frond, rachis or roots can be manipulated to produce new plants (see page 28).

SOWING SPORES Find a clean, draft-free place in which to sow your spores. I generally sow the most difficult or slowest-growing ferns first and the easiest or fastest-growing ferns last; this way, if there are any stray spores, the former will not be tainted by the latter. Sow the spores by lightly tapping them from the packet or off a flat sheet of paper, or by sifting them through lens tissue. Label the culture, making sure to note the name of the fern, date sown, source and any other information you want to remember. The label can be a piece of tape on the outside of the container or a plastic label stuck inside the container; I prefer the latter as the label can then move with the young ferns through the various transplantings.

CARE OF THE SPORE CULTURES A controlled environment with even temperatures and controlled illumination will encourage faster development in many spore cultures. Place the containers under fluorescent lights (anywhere from 6 to 24 inches from the lights) or in indirect natural light. Some species require a period of darkness before being exposed to light. To be on the safe side, I usually let my cultures "rest" for a day in a dim area before transferring them to a lighted growth chamber. Most books recommend leaving artificial lights on 8 to 16 hours daily. I leave the lights on continually with no adverse effects on most of the plants that I grow.

The temperature of the growing area can range from about 55° to 75° F, but

A clump of 'Divisilobum' soft shield fern, *Polystichum setiferum* 'Divisilobum', propagated vegetatively from buds growing on fronds, as shown in the photo at left.

it should remain fairly stable, within five to six degrees. Some temperate species, especially some of the deciduous ones, seem to prefer the cooler end of this range.

Within four to fourteen days you should notice a translucent green film on the surface of the medium, a sign that germination has taken place. The newly emerging gametophytes, which have begun to grow from long, tongue-like threads into the heart-shaped prothalli, are too small to see without magnification. If just enough but not too many spores were sown the culture will have a solid mat of prothalli in two to five months. In a culture that is too sparse, the growing medium is exposed to possible contamination and fertilization between prothalli is difficult. In a very crowded culture, the prothalli may not develop properly and may be more susceptible to fungal invasions.

Crowded cultures can be thinned. Remove the fingernail-sized clumps of prothalli with tweezers, forceps or your fingers. If you have lots of room you can transplant the clumps into a larger container or several small ones. Make a small indentation with a tool or your pinkie finger and gently press each clump into the medium. Sterilizing your tools, even your fingers, in a 5 to 10 percent bleach solution before and between transplantings of different ferns is highly recommended.

After transplanting, mist with distilled or cooled boiled water. The transplanted clumps will continue to grow and once again make a solid mat of prothalli. The length of time required for prothalli to produce sporophytes varies according to species and environmental conditions — it can be anywhere from six to twelve months. If sporophytes are not produced after a reasonable length of time, try flooding the entire culture with a thin film of sterile water for a few hours, then remove any excess not absorbed.

Once sporophytes begin to develop, you may have to thin again. Continue to keep the containers and the mix as sterile as possible because the growing mix will have had to be exposed during various procedures. As they develop more fronds you can gradually uncover the containers by propping open the lids to let in air. Commercial growers tend to transplant in clumps, even the larger ferns, as ferns seems to prefer the "buddy system." Clumps of no more than two to three sporelings are most successful. Once ferns reach roughly 15 to 25 percent of their mature size they can safely be divided into single plants if you desire.

DISEASES AND PESTS Despite all precautions to keep the work area, tools and growing medium sterile, contaminants do sneak in. The close conditions under which spore cultures are kept favors the growth of molds and algae. Check regularly for signs of infection. Blue-green "algae" will turn the opaque prothalli a translucent sooty green that grows darker as the prothalli deteriorate. Furry, dingy white to ashen gray wisps on the prothalli or foliage are caused by gray mold. Cool moist conditions stimulate this mold and an increase in temperature, good air circulation and decrease in humidity will slow it down. As soon as you spot an infection, remove the infected area and at least 1/2 inch of plant tissue beyond that. Fungicides usually slow the progress of these infections but don't cure them. They may also inhibit the growth of the prothalli of some ferns.

Algae, mosses and liverworts do not directly attack the prothalli or sporelings but can impede their development by crowding and shading them. Green ooze, grayish thatch or stringy green strands are probably algae. Remove the algal patches as thoroughly as possible to give the prothalli or sporelings a chance to develop without heavy competition. This procedure may have to be repeated before the sporophytes can hold their own. I have spent many hours pulling the stringy algae from cultures. Mosses and liverworts also should be removed as soon as you spot them. They favor bright light and, like algae, tend to be a problem in older cultures, particularly those with the slower-developing ferns.

A SOILLESS MEDIUM FOR GROWING FERNS FROM SPORES

1 bale fine perlite
1/2 bale peat moss
2 cups 9 to 12 month, timed-release high-nitrogen fertilizer
1/4 cup micronutrients

Lightly moisten the mix while thoroughly combining the ingredients.

Fungus gnats and shore flies are an absolute menace and can cause serious damage in a closed culture. The minute, white, worm-like larvae slither through the upper surface of the medium, destroying vital rhizoids. Adult fungus gnats have light-colored wings and adult shore flies have dark ones. It is important to distinguish between the two because fungus gnat larvae can be controlled by a biological larvicide but shore flies require a toxic treatment not recommended for use around the home. Aphids can be controlled with a mild solution of dishwashing detergent. To avoid damaging your cultures, leave the detergent solution on the fronds for about 30 to 60 minutes and then be sure to spray with sterile water to remove excess soap and aphid bodies.

Prevention is the best pest-management strategy. Use sterile containers, medium and spores and keep yourself and your work area free of contaminants. Wash your hands before and between handling cultures. Make sure your clothing is clean — and don't bounce from outdoor gardening to working on your cultures because you'll have all sorts of microscopic contaminants on your apparel. Consider chemical pesticides and fungicides only as a last resort. Your local cooperative extension agent is the best source of information on which ones to use.

TRUE FROM SPORES OR NOT SO TRUE Even if you've successfully run the course from spores to prothalli to mature sporophytes, you may have another obstacle to contend with — "rogue" spores that have produced plants that you did not intend to grow. As you become experienced you'll be able to recognize these invaders and choose whether to keep them or discard them.

You may also be surprised to discover that some spores produce plants that do not absolutely resemble the parents. Fern species come "true" to their parentage allowing for the normal range of variation within an individual species. Some species reproduce as if they were all cut from the same cookie cutter. Others

THREE EASY WAYS TO PROPAGATE FERNS

You don't have to sow spores to increase your collection of ferns. Vegetative, or asexual, propagation is much simpler. It involves taking parts of a fern or young plants that have grown by a bud directly from the parent fern and planting them. The resulting new plants mature quickly. But there is one drawback to vegetative propagation — you're limited to the plants in your own or a friend's collection, whereas propagation by spores gives you access to a much wider array of ferns from across the country and around the world.

CREEPING RHIZOMES The simplest way to propagate vegetatively is to divide branching rhizomes into separate plants. In ferns with creeping rhizomes, such as hay-scented fern (*Dennstaedtia punctilobula*), many divisions may be possible from a modest clump. You're more likely to have success with a larger division, so make sure that each one has at least one or two growing tips. One notable exception to this rule is Himalayan or evergreen maidenhair fern (*Adiantum venustum*), which thrives when its rhizomes are ruthlessly reduced to mere fragments. Use a clean, sharp knife or pruners to cut divisions. You can also tease apart rhizomes that have become entwined, taking care to salvage as many roots as possible. I find that long creeping rhizomes do best when planted in a loose mix in a low, wide pot instead of a standard taller pot.

PROLIFEROUS BUDS In some species, buds that grow on the frond, rachis or even roots can be manipulated to produce new plants. For best success, in the case of proliferous, or bud-bearing, fronds keep these attached to

exhibit a tremendous ability to produce variations strikingly different from the parent. Some of these variations may come relatively true to type when grown from spores, but others, most notably *Athyrium filix-femina, Asplenium scolopendrium* and *Polystichum setiferum,* may produce some progeny that are not quite true to the original named variety. Even within these species there are exceptions, however. For more information on this intriguing subject, see *The Cultivation and Propagation of British Ferns* by James W. Dyce. Mr. Dyce has been my unflagging mentor for nearly two decades. I hope I have been able to instill in you a fraction of the passion for ferns that he has helped instill in me.

the parent plant while anchoring them to the ground or a pot of soil. This ensures that the frond remains alive and healthy while the new plantlets are developing their own roots and fronds. If you remove the fronds from the parent, be sure to keep them in a humid environment, such as a covered flat or plastic container, while the plantlets develop or the fronds will dry out.

STIPE PROPAGATION Victorian growers were exceedingly creative and discovered some intriguing vegetative propagation techniques. Because some varieties did not produce spores or did not come "true" from spores and rhizome division yielded too limited a number of new plants, they tried potting up old stipe bases severed from the rhizome. There are some reports in the literature of the day that this technique worked with *Dryopteris filix-mas* and *Dryopteris affinis* selections, but I have not tried it. However, I have coaxed old stipe bases of *Asplenium scolopendrium* var. *scolopendrium,* the European hart's-tongue fern, to produce plantlets. If you want to give this a try, cut the stipe bases about 1/4" to 1/2" in length and insert them upside down in a rooting mix. Little green pimples on the upper portion of the section above the soil will form, which will develop into plantlets. You can also lay the pieces on the soil surface, but do be sure to keep the severed stipes in a closed, humid environment. I have even seen plastic bags full of leafed-out stipe bases that never made it from the bag to the rooting container!

I like to think that this phenomenon was discovered when the stipes, lying about on a propagation tray after a prized "scolly" (the affectionate English nickname for hart's-tongue fern) was potted or cleaned up, eventually grew into plants. Moral of the story: Sometimes dubious bits and pieces may have propagation potential and the experience gained from trial and error takes no more than a little patience and space.

HOW TO GROW FERNS

BY NANCY SWELL

FERNS ARE a widely varied group of plants. Their native habitats range from the tropics to the Arctic and from deserts to swamps. They may be coarse or delicate, succulent or filmy, crown forming or creeping, lime lovers or lime intolerant, invasive weeds or virtually impossible to cultivate. One of the first plant groups to adapt to life on land, ferns have since adapted to most conditions and environments, but relatively few are able to contend with direct sunlight and low humidity. Most species need moist soil, high humidity and enough shade to maintain these conditions.

Ferns are essentially wildlings; unlike many of the flowering plants, such as herbaceous perennials, they have not been hybridized for garden conditions. Before you begin your fern garden, observe the ferns growing naturally in your area. Most of these are available commercially. Be sure to place them in your garden where conditions are comparable to those supporting the native ferns in the wild. Be cautious in your selection. If a fern's growth in the wild is rampant, it is likely to be even more so in your garden. If the fern grows only in a specialized habitat, such as moist rock crevices, it may be difficult to grow in the garden. Grow only those plants for which you have the proper conditions. Never collect ferns from the wild. When you buy ferns, look for reputable dealers who state explicitly that their plants are nursery propagated, not collected from the wild. Selected forms with fancy fronds are always nursery propagated.

CHOOSING FERNS The section of the country where you live and garden determines to a large extent the plants you can grow. Most of Florida and the southern coastal areas can grow the tropical ferns that the rest of us can cultivate only under glass or as house plants. Southwest gardeners can grow only those that have adapted to less humidity, while gardeners in the midwest, northeast, mid-atlantic and upper south can grow most woodland types.

Because ferns are essentially wildlings that have not been hybridized for garden use, they need conditions similar to those in their natural habitats. Swamp water fern, *Blechnum serrulatum*, requires moist to wet, acidic and humus-rich soil.

Keep in mind, too, that some ferns have specialized requirements. It's not impossible to grow maidenhairs, hart's tongues or other ferns that prefer an alkaline soil, even if your soil tends toward the acidic; mixing crushed limestone, oyster shell grit or cement rubble in the soil will provide a constant source of lime and improve drainage. If you live in a limestone area and want to grow those that require acid conditions, it is not quite so easy. You can make the planting bed acidic by working lots of peat or humus into the soil, separating it from the subsoil with landscape fabric or a two-inch layer of granite grit and treating the soil with sulfur or ammonium nitrate. The problem is that the water in these areas is likely to be alkaline, and will gradually change the pH of the soil. Under these conditions, it's best to grow ferns that prefer limestone, or those tolerant of alkaline conditions. Most adiantums, aspleniums, polystichums, dryopteris and athyriums will grow in a wide pH range, and the organic material in a well prepared soil will help to buffer the effect of excess acidity or alkalinity.

Many ferns have a natural affinity for rocks. Some, such as polypodies and the walking fern will actually grow on the rock surface; others, such as *Cheilanthes* and the cliff brakes, need exceptionally sharp drainage and more sun. Almost all appreciate the protection of rocks, which help the soil retain moisture and establish a microclimate that is warmer in winter and cooler in summer than the surrounding environment. It's important to know which ferns must have limestone and which require acid conditions. Sandstone and granite rocks are generally the foundation for those needing acid, while limestone or even cement rubble will provide alkalinity. Ferns among rocks should be planted in a well drained but moisture-retentive soil.

WOODLAND FERNS For gardeners in most regions of the country, species adapted to woodland environments are attractive and easy to grow. In most areas, Christmas or sword ferns (*Polystichum* spp.), lady ferns (*Athyrium* spp.) and shield ferns (*Dryopteris* spp.) are commonly found in the wild. These genera contain other non-native species that will grow under similar conditions in the garden. Most prefer a slightly acidic soil with 50 to 75 percent humus, good water retention and excellent drainage.To add humus to your soil, work about 4 inches of coarse compost, rotted manure or fine pine bark into the top 4 to 6 inches. All ferns require ample moisture for growth, as well as a certain amount of humidity to prevent dehydration of their foliage. Established plants of most woodland species are tolerant of periodic dry spells, but that doesn't mean they will survive bone-dry conditions. Only a very few are adapted to life in bogs or really wet conditions. Swamp, bog and streamside ferns such as the osmundas require more water than most woodland ferns.

WHICH FERNS ARE FOR YOU?

FERNS FOR BEGINNERS

Adiantum pedatum
Athyrium filix-femina
Blechnum spicant
Cyrtomium species
Cystopteris species
Deparia acrostichoides
Dryopteris dilatata
Dryopteris erythrosora
Dryopteris expansa
Dryopteris filix-mas
Dryopteris marginalis
Matteuccia struthiopteris
Polystichum acrostichoides
Polystichum munitum
Polystichum setiferum
Thelypteris noveboracensis

FERNS FOR SUN

Athyrium filix-femina
Dennstaedtia punctilobula
Dryopteris filix-mas
Dryopteris ludoviciana
Matteuccia struthiopteris
Onoclea sensibilis
Osmunda cinnamomea
Osmunda regalis
Polystichum setiferum
Sphaeropteris cooperi
Thelypteris kunthii
Woodwardia virginica

FERNS FOR DEEP SHADE

Asplenium rhizophyllum
Blechnum spicant
Cyrtomium falcatum
Dryopteris (evergreen species)
Gymnocarpium species
Osmunda cinnamomea
Polystichum species
Phegopteris species
Woodwardia areolata

FERNS FOR WET SOILS

Athyrium filix-femina
Blechnum serrulatum
Dryopteris celsa
Dryopteris ludoviciana
Macrothelypteris torresiana
Onoclea sensibilis
Osmunda cinnamomea
Osmunda regalis
Thelypteris kunthii
Thelypteris palustris
Woodwardia species

FERNS FOR DRY SOIL

Asplenium platyneuron
Blechnum penna-marina
Cystopteris bulbifera
Dennstaedtia punctilobula
Dryopteris filix-mas
Dryopteris intermedia
Dryopteris marginalis
Osmunda claytoniana
Pentagramma triangularis
Polypodium species
Polystichum species
Phegopteris hexagonoptera
Woodsia obtusa

FERNS FOR ALKALINE SOILS

Adiantum species
Asplenium most species
Cystopteris bulbifera
Diplazium pycnocarpon
Dryopteris carthusiana
Dryopteris dilatata
Dryopteris expansa
Gymnocarpium robertianum
Matteuccia struthiopteris
Osmunda claytoniana
Polystichum aculeatum
Thelypteris palustris

FERNS FOR STRONGLY ACIDIC SOILS

Asplenium platyneuron
Blechnum species
Cyrtomium species
Dennstaedtia punctilobula
Dryopteris campyloptera
Dryopteris cycadina
Dryopteris ludoviciana
Gymnocarpium dryopteris
Osmunda cinnamomea
Osmunda regalis
Polypodium species
Polystichum species
Phegopteris connectilis
Thelypteris species
Woodsia obtusa
Woodwardia species

Woodland ferns do best in high or dappled shade. The open shade of mature trees or the north side of the house or a wall, open to the sky, provide nearly ideal light conditions. Most woodland ferns will adapt to relatively low light levels, but no ferns thrive in deep shade. Evergreen species are the most tolerant of low light levels. Generally, plants will tolerate more sun and less water in the northern part of their range. The stronger the sun, the greater the need for water; conversely, the more water available, the more sun they will take.

The nutritional needs of ferns are generally met with compost or the breakdown of leaves. Small size and slow growth are more likely to be caused by limited water than lack of food. In fact, ferns are sensitive to excess fertilizer; quick-release inorganic fertilizers are likely to burn the roots. If supplemental feeding is needed, use well rotted manure, fish emulsion or other slow-release organic food. Wind protection prevents the breakage of brittle fronds and reduces dehydration. While shelter is an advantage, the lowest, most sheltered spot is also probably a frost pocket which can delay spring growth, and result in early and late frost damage to deciduous ferns and winter-kill of species with borderline hardiness.

PLANTING FERNS The best time to plant varies according to geographic location. Spring planting is preferable where winters are cold and wet. If ferns are planted late in the season in these areas, the roots could very well rot before they are established. Alternate freezing and thawing may heave the rhizomes from the soil, breaking young roots and exposing them, making them prone to desiccation. In warmer climates, fall planting is preferable because the plant has time to establish itself before the stresses of summer heat and drought. If you move or plant a fern that is actively growing, cut the fronds back by half to reduce stress from water loss and help it get established. New fronds usually will be produced as soon as the plant has enough roots to support them.

To move a fern, dig a generous root ball, especially if the plant is in active growth. Next, dig a hole the same depth as the root ball and place the plant in the hole, water well, fill in the sides with good soil and firm the soil around the plant. If the job is well done, the fern may never know it has been moved.

Many ferns available for sale are grown in quart size or larger pots. These are either mature size or will grow to maturity in a year or two.To plant a potted fern, knock the plant out of the pot and gently shake or tease the roots apart. It is important to remove excess potting soil, especially if it differs significantly from the soil in your garden. Potting soils are often light and peaty and will dry out faster than the surrounding soil. This may leave the newly planted fern dry and wilted even though the surrounding soil is moist. To rectify the situation, spread out the roots, mix some of the potting soil into the root area, water well and fill in the planting hole with good soil. Keep newly planted ferns well watered for the first growing season while they are becoming established.

Never let plants growing in 4-inch or smaller pots dry out until they reach a mature size and are well established. Plant them in well prepared soil in a protected area. It is often easier to pot them up for special care. Add fine pine bark to any good potting mix to improve drainage. Do not feed until they are growing well. If the fern requires alkaline conditions, you can add a tablespoon of ground limestone to a gallon of planting mix.

Ferns sold by mail may have been removed from their pots and put in plastic bags or they may be almost bare rooted. When you unpack the plants make sure that the growing tip has not been damaged during shipping. If it has been broken or has rotted, the fern will probably not recover and the shipper should be notified immediately. Depending on size, either pot the fern or plant it in a protected spot and keep it well watered until it has had a chance to establish itself. If the roots seem at all dry, set the plant in water for one to two hours while you are preparing the planting area.

GROWING TIPS

Both fern fronds and roots grow directly from the stem, which is also known as the rhizome. All new growth is produced at the stem tip, and if it is damaged the entire plant may be killed. The roots grow at the base of the fronds, or on the lower side of creeping rhizomes. In all ferns they are close to the surface and easily disturbed.

Upright-growing rhizomes form a distinct crown consisting of the tightly coiled croziers at the soil surface, which grow in spring into a whorl of fronds that radiate from the center like a vase. These may grow out of the ground to form small trunks. The roots that grow at the base of the fronds are then exposed to the air and can dry out. If crowns lift themselves out of the soil they need to be replanted to return them to soil level. Adding one to two inches of mulch each year may make replanting unnecessary.

Rakes, hoes and feet do not belong in the fern garden. Surface roots, tightly coiled croziers and developing fiddleheads are too easily damaged. Leave a place to walk, and remove by hand winter-burned evergreen fronds and any other garden debris before the fiddleheads begin to unfurl in spring.

Some ferns may be purchased as small bare rooted plants packed in dry peat moss in a plastic bag. In theory, there is enough humidity in the bag to prevent desiccation of the plant; in practice, ferns do not appreciate being bare rooted, and while they will certainly rot if they are enclosed with wet peat, they are generally dry enough to need a recovery period. Unless you can actually see signs of active growth such as a crozier beginning to uncurl, bare rooted plants are best avoided. Often the growing tip has been damaged by handling, or the peat has become completely dry. If you do try ferns sold this way, soak them in water for a couple of hours and pot them using a good, well draining potting mix. Be careful to keep the growing tips at or above soil level. Keep well watered and transplant to the garden after they have become established. Another disadvantage of ferns sold bare root is that they are frequently dug up from the wild.

How far apart should you plant your ferns? Spacing depends on form, size and type of growth. Crown formers with upright rhizomes and vase-shaped form spread slowly and show to best advantage as a single crown. Goldie's fern and some of the larger growing polystichums and osmundas may need three feet or more between plants. Oak and beech ferns spread quickly and can be planted fairly far apart. Hay-scented, New York and Virginia chain fern are even more rampant spreaders, and the ostrich fern, which spreads by far-ranging runners, is best planted in an area where it can be controlled.

CARING FOR FERNS If you choose plants suited to your growing conditions and practice good gardening hygiene, removing debris that may harbor pests, you may seldom have to deal with diseases or pests. Slugs and snails tend to be the most common problems; they are voracious eaters that thrive under the same conditions as ferns. Slug baits containing metaldehyde are effective, but they are toxic and especially hazardous to children and pets. Various nontoxic baits and traps are safer: Dishes of beer sunk to soil level are effective. Slugs will also collect under overturned grapefruit shells and can then be dropped into denatured alcohol for the coup de grace. Ferns are quite sensitive to insecticides. If you must use a chemical poison, test it on a few plants. Avoid the liquid emulsion sprays, as they contain oils that damage ferns. Use dusts or sprays made from wettable powders, reducing the recommended dosage by one half.

To prevent disease, start with healthy plants. Keep the crown of the plant above the soil, and don't cover it with mulch. Avoid overwatering and space the plants far enough apart for adequate air circulation. Mulching with fine pine bark, pine needles or a fairly coarse compost will help keep the soil moist, prevent weeds or at least make them easier to pull and provide essentially all the nutrients your ferns need. Replenish the mulch each year to compensate for the tendency of certain athyriums or dryopteris to raise their crowns above soil level.

LANDSCAPING WITH FERNS

BY NANCY SWELL

ERNS, all the rage during the Victorian era, were forgotten for decades. Today, natural landscaping is the hottest trend in gardening since the English-style herbaceous border, and these wildlings are making a comeback. Yet ferns have a place in almost any kind of garden. In traditional formal gardens, ferns are perfect as

Western sword fern, *Polystichum munitum*, and Anderson's holly fern, *P. andersonii*, combined with hosta and London-pride, accent carpets of moss on a boulder-strewn slope.

groundcovers, foundation plantings, accents, specimen plants and underplantings for shrubs. Ferns are a natural element of the woodland garden. Here is found the partial shade, wind protection and increased humidity that enables most ferns to thrive. Indeed, woodlands are the natural habitats of many of our ferns. For world-weary humans, woodland gardens provide a quiet retreat from the stresses of everyday life.

WOODLAND GARDENS If you want to recreate a patch of native forest in your yard or embellish a remnant that's already there, select ferns indigenous to your area. At a minimum, select species suited to the conditions in your garden. Broad and narrow beech ferns, oak fern and polypodies are graceful ground covers, wandering happily through the humus-rich litter of the woodland floor. These are not for accents; they don't stay where they're put, but rather naturalize quickly to create a delightful unplanned effect. New York and hay-scented ferns not only wander but also tend to take over their area. They are most useful in larger areas where there are no delicate treasures to be overgrown.

FERNS AS ACCENTS Consider using some strong growing accents along woodland paths to help lead the eye from one place to another. Most of the dryopteris can be used for this purpose; good choices include the majestic Goldie's fern, the dark-leaved autumn fern, the blue-green, vase-shaped marginal woods fern and the varied forms of the male fern. The elegant maidenhair is a must-have. The evergreen Christmas fern, the soft shield fern and the tassel fern are lovely evergreen ferns. Add to this list the Japanese painted fern with its bright variegated foliage, and you can create an unforgettable picture. Any or all of these can also be used in a shaded flower border with good soil and adequate moisture. They provide interesting texture and unifying shades of green to the border. Use the vigorous lady ferns with caution. Most of their ruffled, fringed or otherwise modified cultivars are less invasive and very interesting in their own right, though they may be a bit exotic for a naturalized effect.

STREAMSIDE GARDENS If you're lucky enough to have a stream running through your property, or if you can develop a moist area near a pool, the decorative possibilities of ferns are exceptional. Here you can grow the large and stately royal fern, the cinnamon fern and the ostrich fern. With enough water, these grow big, and this must be taken into consideration. The ostrich fern also

Right: An elegant combination for the natural garden—southern maidenhair fern, native to the Southeast and west to southern California, and wild ginger, whose native habitat ranges from New Brunswick south to North Carolina and Missouri.

spreads by runners and can outgrow its area unless it is restrained. Sensitive fern and the Virginia chain fern may also overstep their bounds under these conditions. As long as there is good drainage, any of the woodland ferns are also suitable for streamside or poolside plantings. In fact, they tend to grow bigger and better with the extra water. As usual, maidenhairs are essential. They are the true grace notes of the garden.

ROCK FERNS Try fitting some of the smaller ferns into the crevices in, on or along walls and steps. These specialized ferns require extra drainage and may need to be isolated from larger or faster-growing plants. If mortar has been used,

(continues on page 42)

FERNS IN CONTAINERS

Ferns with special requirements are often easier to grow if they are isolated in a container.

There are many reasons to grow hardy ferns in containers. A plant in a container is portable. It may be placed wherever an accent or garden feature is needed, regardless of soil conditions. Plants in pots are often essential in paved areas such as patios, and are just as useful where tree root competition makes it next to impossible for anything to grow. Pots submerged in mulch beds can be used for variable displays. These are particularly effective around garden pools. Another advantage is that less hardy varieties can be used in the displays during the growing season, then protected over the winter. Ferns in pots can temporarily fill in blank spots in the flower border. Pots can also be placed on pedestals, hung from trees or perched on fences.

It is much easier to meet the special requirements of some ferns if they are isolated in a container. Lip ferns need a quick-draining acidic soil and more light than most ferns. Cliff brakes need bright light and an alkaline soil. Most of the small aspleniums, including the walking fern and its hybrids, need a soil that drains well but holds moisture. More than anything else, the aspleniums need protection from slugs and snails and from competition from larger plants. You can create small rock gardens in hypertufa troughs (rustic, porous containers made of peat, perlite and Portland cement). These make attractive display gardens for the smallest of the ferns, and the location and planting mix can be adjusted to meet any requirements.

The best potting mixes are based on either loamy soil or soil substitutes such as peat moss or pine bark. No matter what type, a mix must be compact enough to hold the plants in position, free draining but moisture retentive, fertile and open enough so that air can reach the roots. Potting mixes must not carry disease, weed seeds or pests. Choosing soil mixes is not an exact science; there are probably as many mixes as there are growers and gardeners, each of whom modifies his basic mix according to the requirements of the species being grown.

The following is a typical soil-based mix:

ONE PART GOOD GARDEN SOIL
ONE PART COARSE WASHED SAND
TWO OR MORE PARTS ORGANIC MATERIAL SUCH AS PEAT MOSS, COMPOSTED LEAVES OR FINE PINE BARK.

If you start with a good loamy soil, this mix will grow the best plants of all. The two major drawbacks of soil-based mixes are the difficulty in finding good soil and the need to sterilize it. Sterilized soil is especially important for sporelings and young transplants. For lime-loving ferns, add one ounce or more ground limestone per cubic foot of soil mix. If you have difficulty finding coarse sand, you can use "starter grit" found in feed stores.

The following are soilless mixes based on peat moss:

ONE PART SAND
ONE PART PEAT MOSS

For a lighter mix, try:

TWO PARTS PEAT MOSS
ONE PART VERMICULITE
ONE PART PERLITE

Potting mixes for ferns can also be based on pine bark. Start with a finely ground bark (it should pass through a 1/2-inch sieve) that has been wet down and composted for about a month. After composting, mix as follows:

THREE PARTS BARK
ONE PART COARSE SAND
ONE PART PEAT MOSS

Soilless mixes must have all nutrients added to them, including micronutrients. To three cubic feet of mix, add five ounces of a slow-release fertilizer, one ounce of superphosphate, two ounces of lime, two ounces of gypsum and 1-1/2 teaspoons of micronutrient.

If you buy an already prepared potting mix, make sure it has the qualities listed above.

Plants in containers may need to be fed more often than plants in the ground because frequent watering causes most nutrients to leach out of the soil. Use soluble fertilizer at half the strength recommended for other house plants. Make sure that the potting mix drains freely to avoid salt buildup.

ferns preferring an alkaline soil are the best choice. Walls often create a microclimate that enables you to grow ferns that are only marginally hardy in your area. Particularly appropriate are the spleenworts, polypodies, lip ferns and perhaps the cliff brake. English hart's tongue (much easier to grow than our American native) is a memorable sight when planted in walls and steps.

Any of the accent ferns recommended above for use along woodland paths can be planted against a rock or boulder or wall to catch the eye and trace an interesting pattern against its background.

Ostrich fern, *Matteuccia struthiopteris*, has great presence. The plants grow 3 to 5 feet tall. Use them along foundations or in drifts in the woodland garden. Clumps of ostrich fern spread rapidly.

ENCYCLOPEDIA OF FERNS FOR THE HOME GARDEN

HOW THE ENCYCLOPEDIA IS ORGANIZED:

The ferns that lead off each encyclopedia entry are the most popular or most widely available species of their genus. A handful of genera, such as *Athyrium* and *Dryopteris*, include so many species grown in gardens that it was useful to divide them into more than one encyclopedia entry. The ferns in these multiple entries are grouped according to obvious physical characteristics, such as the degree of dissection of the frond, or whether they are evergreen or deciduous.

Adiantum pedatum
NORTHERN
MAIDENHAIR
FERN

NATIVE HABITAT: Eastern and central North America from Southern Canada to the Gulf Coast

HARDINESS ZONE: 3 to 9

OUTSTANDING FEATURES: A unique, airy fern with fan-shaped fronds held on thin black stipes above a creeping rhizome. Each horseshoe-shaped rachis bears long and narrow branches of overlapping shell-shaped pinnae. The delicate, pale green fronds emerge in early spring and turn deep blue-green as they mature. Maidenhairs grow in tight clumps that spread to form broad patches. Spores are borne on the outside margins of the pinnae and are covered by false indusia formed by the folded edge of the pinnae. Maidenhair ferns grow one to three feet tall. The deciduous fronds are 3-pinnate.

GARDEN USE: Plant maidenhair ferns in groups or drifts in woodland gardens, under shrubs and flowering trees or with other ferns as a foundation planting. Combine the delicate pink fiddleheads with bulbs and spring wildflowers.

HOW TO GROW: Prefers moist, neutral, humus-rich soil in partial to full shade. Plants tolerate some drought. Divide clumps when they become so congested that you cannot see the individual form of the fronds.

CULTIVARS AND RELATED SPECIES

A. aleuticum Five Finger Maidenhair, Western Maidenhair — Similar to Northern maidenhair with 2 to 3-foot stiff fronds sporting an elongated central pinna resembling an extended finger. Native to Western North America and Japan. Deciduous, 2-pinnate. Zones 4 to 9.

'Japonicum' — Similar to the above but with 1- to 2-foot reddish tinged fronds. Native to Japan. Deciduous, 2-pinnate. Zones 4 to 8.

A. aleuticum dwarf ecotype. Dwarf Western Maidenhair — This diminutive fern is a replica in miniature of its full-sized relative. Plants grow 3 to 9 inches tall in tight clumps. Zones 5 to 8.

A. capillus-veneris Southern Maidenhair — An attractive fern bearing 1- to 2-foot, cascading, triangular fronds with bright green, fan-shaped leaflets. Requires moist, limy soils and often grows on wet rocks. Native to the Southeastern and Gulf States, the Rockies as far north as Utah and west to California. Deciduous, 1-pinnate upper fronds, 2-pinnate lower. Zones 6 to 9.

Asplenium scolopendrium
(Phyllitis scolopendrium)

Hart's-tongue Fern

NATIVE HABITAT: In North America this fern grows only in a few isolated limestone sinks in Ontario, Michigan, New York, Alabama and Tennessee. In Europe, hart's-tongue is widespread and common.

HARDINESS ZONE: 6 to 8

OUTSTANDING FEATURES: Hart's-tongue is unique among hardy ferns because it has undivided, leathery, strap-like fronds that arise like a vase from a thick rhizome. Linear sori with two marginal indusia are borne in pairs along the veins of fertile fronds. Mature plants may reach 2 feet in height. The evergreen fronds are entire.

GARDEN USE: Use hart's-tongue as an accent among woodland plants or in stone walls and steps. It grows well in containers and troughs. Plants will self-sow under ideal conditions.

HOW TO GROW: The American hart's-tongue (var. *americanum*) is rare in the wild and difficult to grow. Plant European hart's-tongue (var. *scolopendrium*) in moist, neutral or alkaline humus-rich soil in sun or shade. Plants often grow in wall crevices and among rocks. Add concrete rubble or oyster shells to sweeten acidic soils. Slugs and snails may devour the fronds.

CULTIVARS AND RELATED SPECIES

'Cristatum' — This variable selection has 6- to 12-inch fronds with crests and tassels.

'Laceratum Kaye' — A 6-inch dwarf selection that has fronds with jagged, crested edges.

'Marginatum'— This 8- to 12-inch selection has narrow fronds with wavy margins and occasional crested tips.

'Undulatum'— A popular selection with 12-inch, ruffled fronds.

A cultivar with ruffled fronds

Asplenium trichomanes
Maidenhair
Spleenwort

NATIVE HABITAT: Throughout North America, Europe and Asia

HARDINESS ZONE: 3 to 9

OUTSTANDING FEATURES: This enchanting rock fern forms dense, tufted rosettes of deep green fronds from a short rhizome. Each slender frond is lined with a paired row of small, rounded pinnae along a black stipe. Linear sori with narrow indusia are borne along the veins of fertile pinnae. Plants grow 4 to 6 inches tall. The evergreen fronds are 1-pinnate.

GARDEN USE: Use this delicate fern in crevices in walls and steps or in a scree or rock garden. Plants grow well in troughs and other containers.

HOW TO GROW: Maidenhair spleenwort is one of the easiest of the rock ferns to grow. Plant in moist, neutral, humus-rich soil among rocks or carefully insert the roots and rhizome into pockets of soil in an unmortared wall. Self-sown sporelings will appear wherever conditions are favorable.

CULTIVARS AND RELATED SPECIES

A. **x** *ebenoides* Scott's Spleenwort— An attractive fern with deeply lobed, 10 to 20-inch, lance-shaped fronds from a creeping rhizome. Give plants the same growing conditions as maidenhair spleenwort. May be short-lived in cultivation, but plants grow well in containers. Slugs may devour the fronds. This species is a rare, naturally occurring sterile hybrid of *A. platyneuron* and *A. rhizophyllum* and is found from Vermont to Illinois and south to Alabama and Arkansas. Evergreen, pinnatifid to 1-pinnate. Zones 4 to 9.

A. platyneuron Ebony Spleenwort— This popular fern produces slightly dimorphic fronds from a creeping, crown-forming rhizome. The sterile fronds are arching to flattened while the 12- to 20-inch, herringbone-shaped fertile fronds stand strictly upright. Plants require moist but well-drained, acidic, humus-rich to rocky soil in light to full shade. Plants also grow on rocks. Native to eastern North America. Evergreen, 1-pinnate. Zones 3 to 9.

A. rhizophyllum (*Camptosorus rhizophyllus*) Walking Fern— A fascinating fern that "walks" over rocks by rooting and forming a new plant at the tip of each 2- to 8-inch, lance-shaped frond. Walking fern is difficult to grow. Plant in moist, humus-rich soil on limestone rocks. Slugs may devour the fronds. Native in limestone regions from Quebec and Ontario south to Georgia and Oklahoma. Evergreen, entire. Zones 4 to 8.

Athyrium filix-femina

Lady Fern

NATIVE HABITAT: Throughout North and Central America, Europe, Asia, India and Africa

HARDINESS ZONE: 3 to 8

OUTSTANDING FEATURES: The intricately cut fronds of lady fern are the ideal picture of "fernyness." Billowing clusters of lacy fronds arise from the creeping rhizome. Linear sori with thin, crescent-shaped indusia are borne along the veins of the pinnules of fertile fronds. Plants grow 1 to 3 feet tall. The western subspecies may grow to 4 feet. The deciduous fronds are 2-pinnate pinnatifid.

GARDEN USE: Lady fern forms dense leafy clumps that combine well with bold perennials such as hostas and ligularias and vertical plants such as iris and black cohosh (*Cimicifuga racemosa.*). Plant them in drifts or as a groundcover in moist sites. Clumps spread rapidly and may overrun delicate plants.

HOW TO GROW: Plant lady ferns in moist to wet, neutral to acidic, humus-rich soil in partial to full shade. Plants in constantly moist soil tolerate sun. Divide overgrown clumps in spring or fall to control their spread. If fronds look ratty or tattered, cut them to the ground and fresh fronds will soon appear.

CULTIVARS AND RELATED SPECIES

'Fancy Fronds'— A dwarf selection with congested, fringed pinnae and an apical crest.

'Fieldiae'— Has tall narrow fronds with paired pinnae that form crosses.

'Frizelliae'— This cultivar has linear fronds with small, round pinnae.

'Plumosum Axminster'— A selection with deeply dissected fronds that resemble those of soft shield fern.

'Victoriae'— A beautiful selection with narrow pinnae that taper to crested tips. The top of the frond is also crested.

A. niponicum 'Pictum' Japanese Painted Fern— One of the showiest ferns for the garden. Silvery gray fronds with red veins form dense clumps from creeping rhizomes. The fronds resemble those of lady fern in shape but are only 1 to 2 feet tall. Give plants moist, neutral to moderately acidic soil in light to partial shade; deep shade in warmer zones. Native to China, Korea and Japan. Deciduous, 2-pinnate. Zones 4 to 8.

A. otophorum English Painted Fern— An attractive fern new to cultivation in North America. Leathery, triangular fronds emerge chartreuse and mature to deep blue-green with red rachises and veins. Plants grow 1 to 2 feet tall and form open clumps from stout rhizomes. Give plants moist, neutral soil in partial to full shade. Native to China, Korea and Japan. Deciduous, 2-pinnate. Zones 4 to 8.

Blechnum spicant

Deer Fern

NATIVE HABITAT: Pacific Northwest from Alaska to northern California, Europe and Asia

HARDINESS ZONE: 6 to 8

OUTSTANDING FEATURES: Deer fern sports tall, narrow, lance-shaped evergreen fronds that arise in a vase shape from a stout rhizome. This dimorphic fern has spreading pinnatifid sterile fronds and upright fertile fronds with the pinnae flattened like stair steps. Pairs of sori run the entire length of the fertile pinnae on either side of the midvein. Plants grow 2 to 3 feet tall. The evergreen fronds are 1-pinnate.

GARDEN USE: This distinctive fern is best used as an accent alongside a rotting stump or garden feature such as a fountain or statue. Plant deer ferns among low groundcover plants such as wild gingers, bunchberry and sweet woodruff or in a carpet of showy spring flowers such as trilliums and foamflowers. The persistent fronds are a valuable addition to the winter garden.

HOW TO GROW: Plant deer fern in moist, acidic, humus-rich soil in partial to full shade. Protect plants from hot dry breezes. Stately mature clumps seldom need division.

CULTIVARS AND RELATED SPECIES

'Crispum' Crisped Deer Fern — This cultivar has fronds with inrolled, stiff pinnae.

'Redwoods Giant' Redwoods Deer Fern — A robust form with wider fronds.

B. serrulatum Swamp Water Fern— A colony-forming fern that produces broad patches of erect 2- to 3 1/2-foot fronds from a stout, subterranean rhizome. New fronds are pink-tinged and mature to bright green. Plants prefer moist to wet, acidic, humus-rich soil in sun or shade. Native to South America, Australia and Malaysia. Slightly dimorphic, evergreen, 1-pinnate. Zones 9 to 11.

B. penna-marina Little Hard Fern— This compact, fast-creeping fern produces upright fertile fronds that are only 4 to 8 inches tall. They emerge with a rosy tinge in spring and darken to dull green. In autumn they turn chocolate brown and persist through the winter. The smaller sterile fronds lie flat on the ground. Plant in well-drained, humus-rich soil in light to partial shade. Native to Australia, New Zealand and South America. Dimorphic, evergreen, 1-pinnate. Zones 7 to 9.

Cyrtomium falcatum
HOLLY FERN

NATIVE HABITAT: Japan, Korea and China

HARDINESS ZONE: 8 to 11

OUTSTANDING FEATURES: The coarse, leathery evergreen fronds of holly fern make it a favorite for gardens, especially in hot climates where other ferns do not thrive. The stiff, arching fronds have wide scythe-shaped pinnae that arise in an open vase shape from a stout, scaly rhizome. The rounded sori with ragged indusia are scattered over the underside of the pinnae of the fertile fronds. Plants grow 1- 1/2 to 2 feet tall. The evergreen fronds are 1-pinnate.

GARDEN USE: Plant holly ferns singly as accents among groundcovers or in drifts with perennials, shrubs and trees. They are excellent as foundation plants alone or combined with flowering shrubs such as azaleas and rhododendrons. The glossy foliage catches light to brighten up shaded spots.

HOW TO GROW: Plant holly ferns in moist, acidic, humus-rich soil in sun or shade. In colder zones fronds may be damaged by dry winter winds. Cut damaged fronds to the ground in spring.

CULTIVARS AND RELATED SPECIES

C. fortunei Holly Fern— This fern resembles *C. falcatum* but has narrower, more erect fronds. Growth requirements are the same. Plants are native to Japan, China and Korea. Evergreen, 1-pinnate. Zones 6 to 11.

C. fortunei grows next to glossy-leaved European ginger in a shady border.

Cystopteris fragilis
FRAGILE FERN

NATIVE HABITAT: Throughout most of North America except the Southeast. Also Europe and Asia

HARDINESS ZONE: 1 to 11

OUTSTANDING FEATURES: Fragile fern is a charming little creeper that sends up frilly, bright green fronds in early spring. Plants form an open carpet from creeping rhizomes but are never invasive. The lance-shaped fronds may wither during summer drought but resprout with the return of cool, wet weather. The rounded sori are partially covered with a thin indusium and are sparsely scattered over the pinnae of the fertile fronds. Plants grow 6 to 10 inches tall. The deciduous fronds are 2-pinnate.

GARDEN USE: Combine fragile fern with spring wildflowers, bulbs and larger ferns where its early emerging fronds lend an airy texture. Take advantage of the spreading habit to cover ground shared by ephemeral plants that go dormant after flowering or as an underplanting for shrubs.

HOW TO GROW: Plant fragile fern in moist, neutral to acidic soil in partial to full shade. Plants also grow well in stone walls. In dry soils, plants go dormant but are not damaged. Overgrown clumps are easily divided in early spring or fall.

CULTIVARS AND RELATED SPECIES

C. bulbifera Bulblet Bladder Fern— A fecund fern with elongated, 12-inch, lance-shaped fronds that produce small bulbils along the rachis and midveins. These bulbils detach and form new plants with lightning speed. The lacy fronds are produced along the creeping rhizome. Plants thrive in rocky, neutral soil and crevices of limestone rocks in partial to full shade. Native to Eastern and Central North America. Deciduous, 2- to 3-pinnate. Zones 3 to 7.

C. protrusa Lowland Fragile Fern, Brittle Fern— This fern closely resembles fragile fern but the growing tip of the rhizome extends an inch or so beyond the last mature frond. The range of lowland fragile fern overlaps with that of fragile fern in Eastern North America. Deciduous, 2-pinnate to 2-pinnate pinnatifid. Zones 4 to 8.

Dennstaedtia punctilobula
HAY-SCENTED FERN

NATIVE HABITAT: Eastern North America from Nova Scotia to Arkansas and Georgia

HARDINESS ZONE: 4 to 7

OUTSTANDING FEATURES: Hay-scented fern is a fast-spreading groundcover that produces a thick mat of bright green, elongated, flexible fronds from a thin, creeping rhizome. The crushed fronds emit the fragrance of freshly mown hay, hence the common name. In autumn, the aging fronds turn soft yellow in color. Rounded sori with cup-shaped indusia are borne in the sinuses of the pinnae segments of the fertile fronds. Plants grow 10 to 18 inches tall. The deciduous fronds are 2-pinnate.

GARDEN USE: Use hay-scented fern where an elegant but tough groundcover is needed. Plants grow under trees and shrubs, among rocks and in poor sandy soil. They even tolerate salt spray. Avoid combining them with delicate plants which may be swamped by the fern's exuberant growth.

HOW TO GROW: Plant hay-scented ferns in moist, neutral to acidic, average to humus-rich soil in sun or shade. Plants in full sun may go dormant if soil becomes too dry. Divide overgrown plants in fall.

CULTIVARS AND RELATED SPECIES

D. bipinnata Cuplet Fern— This somewhat frost-tender fern produces huge 6- to 10-foot fronds from a creeping rhizome. Give plants moist to wet, humus-rich soil in partial to full shade. Native to Central and South America as well as Florida, where it may have escaped cultivation. Deciduous, 3-pinnate pinnatifid. Zones 10 to 11.

Hay-scented fern with phlox

Dicksonia antarctica

Soft Tree Fern

NATIVE HABITAT: Australia

HARDINESS ZONE: 9 to 11

OUTSTANDING FEATURES: This impressive fern is widely grown wherever it is hardy. The broad spreading crown is composed of many 6- to 8-foot, stiff, deep green fronds supported by a stout trunk. Marginal spherical sori are covered by a shell-shaped structure composed of an indusium and the pinnule margin. Plants grow 8 to 25 feet tall. The evergreen fronds are 2-pinnate pinnatifid.

GARDEN USE: Plant soft tree fern as a focal point or accent in a protected courtyard or where dense trees and shrubs block strong winds. This imposing fern creates a lush tropical feel in frost-free gardens. Grow them in containers in colder zones.

HOW TO GROW: Plant soft tree fern in constantly moist, well-drained, humus-rich soil in light to full shade. They are easily transplanted, even when mature. Top dress annually with composted manure. Protect plants from warm, dry winds.

Soft tree ferns used as accents in an island planting. They grow 8 to 25 feet tall.

Diplazium pycnocarpon
(Athyrium pycnocarpon)

GLADE FERN,
NARROW LEAF SPLEENWORT

NATIVE HABITAT: Eastern and central North America

HARDINESS ZONE: 4 to 8

OUTSTANDING FEATURES: Glade fern is an architectural gem for the shade garden. The deep green, arching fronds have undivided lance-shaped pinnae that resemble sword ferns. The fronds are clustered along the creeping rhizome. The fronds are slightly dimorphic. Long straight sori with thin indusia are borne along the veins of the fertile pinnae. Plants grow 1 to 3 feet tall. The deciduous fronds are 1-pinnate.

GARDEN USE: Use glade ferns in drifts with wildflowers and bold-leaved plants such as hostas. They combine well with the strap-like leaves of Siberian iris and the spiky inflorescences of foxgloves and astilbes. The russet autumn fronds are a nice accent with evergreen ferns.

HOW TO GROW: Plant glade fern in constantly moist, neutral, humus-rich soil in partial to full shade. Fronds turn brown quickly if soil gets too dry. The plants spread rapidly. Divide overgrown clumps in spring or fall.

CULTIVARS AND RELATED SPECIES

Deparia acrostichoides (*Athyrium thelypteroides*) Silvery Glade Fern, Silvery Spleenwort — This attractive fern is often overlooked in the wild because it resembles other 2-pinnate ferns. In the garden, plants form robust 2- to 3-foot leafy clumps that remain attractive all season. Fronds turn straw-colored in fall. Plants require constant moisture and neutral to acidic soil for best growth. They tolerate considerable sun if the soil stays moist. Native from Nova Scotia and Ontario south to Georgia and Arkansas. Dimorphic, deciduous, 2-pinnate pinnatifid. Zones 4 to 8.

Deparia acrostichoides

Dryopteris carthusiana

Spinulose Wood Fern, Shield Fern

photo: D. intermedia

NATIVE HABITAT: From Hudson Bay and Alaska south to South Carolina, Missouri and Washington

HARDINESS ZONE: 2 to 7

OUTSTANDING FEATURES: Spinulose wood fern has glossy, deeply dissected fronds that taper toward the tip from a pair of triangular basal pinnae. The fronds emerge in an arching vase shape from an upright, crown-forming rhizome. Rounded sori are covered with shield-shaped indusia that give the genus *Dryopteris* the common name of shield fern. The rhizomes and stipes of most species are covered with papery scales. Plants grow 1- 1/2 to 2- 1/2 feet tall. The mostly evergreen fronds are 2 to 3-pinnate.

GARDEN USE: All wood ferns are elegant garden denizens. Use spinulose wood fern as an accent in moist-soil gardens with primroses, iris and wildflowers. Although evergreen, the fronds collapse after a hard freeze, rendering them ineffective in the winter landscape.

HOW TO GROW: Plant spinulose wood fern in constantly moist, neutral to acidic, humus-rich soil in partial to full shade. Plants are extremely long lived and need no division.

CULTIVARS AND RELATED SPECIES

D. campyloptera Mountain Wood Fern— This fern is similar to the above but has broad, triangular fronds 2 to 3 feet long. Plants require constantly moist, acidic, humus-rich soil in partial to full shade and are restricted to cool areas of the Northeast or high mountains in the Appalachian chain. Evergreen, 2 to 3-pinnate. Zones 4 to 6.

D. expansa Northern Wood Fern— A very variable species. The deep green, 2- to 3-foot fronds are triangular and form a spreading vase. Plants require moist, neutral to acidic, humus-rich soil in partial to full shade. Native to Northern North America, Europe, Asia and South Africa. Evergreen, 2-pinnate pinnatifid to 3-pinnate. Zones 3 to 8.

D. dilatata Broad Wood Fern—Similar to *D. expansa*. Several notable cultivars.

'Crispa Whiteside' Crisped Broad Wood Fern— This cultivar forms an almost drooping vase of fronds with crisped pinnae.

'Jimmy Dyce'— A cultivar with stiff, erect fronds to 2 feet tall.

D. intermedia Fancy Fern, Intermediate Wood Fern— A tough fern often confused with spinulose wood fern but distinguished by its shorter pinnules and deeply dissected, fully evergreen, non-glossy fronds. Fancy fern is also quite drought tolerant. It is common from southern Canada south to Georgia and Missouri. Plants grow 1 -1/2 to 2 -1/2 feet tall. Evergreen, 2-pinnate pinnatifid to 3-pinnate. Zones 3 to 8.

Dryopteris filix-mas
MALE FERN

NATIVE HABITAT: Northern North America south to Vermont, South Dakota and California. Also Europe and Asia

HARDINESS ZONE: 3 to 9

OUTSTANDING FEATURES: Male fern has stiff, lustrous, dark green fronds that form a flattened vase from a crown-forming rhizome. The leathery, lance-shaped fronds taper at both ends. Rounded sori with shield-shaded indusia are borne near the veins of the narrow, dagger-like fertile pinnules. Many crested and tasseled forms are available. Most are of European origin. Plants grow 2 to 3 feet tall. The evergreen fonds are 1-pinnate pinnatifid to 2-pinnate.

GARDEN USE: Male ferns are striking accent plants for moist, shaded gardens. Position them next to stumps, logs or tree trunks for dramatic effect. Use them in mass plantings with flowering shrubs or along a foundation. They are excellent foliage plants for perennial borders. The fancy-leaved selections are interesting additions to gardens.

HOW TO GROW: Plant male ferns in moist, well drained, acidic, humus-rich soil in sun or shade. Shade is mandatory in warmer zones. Plants get large when mature, so leave ample room when setting them out.

CULTIVARS AND RELATED SPECIES

'Barnesii'— This cultivar has narrow, upright, ruffled fronds.

'Cristata Martindale'— A frilled selection with crested pinnae and a terminal crest at the end of the frond.

'Grandiceps'— This 3-foot tall selection has a tasseled crest and pinna tips.

'Linearis Polydactyla'— A cultivar with fine-textured, crested, linear pinnules on 3- to 4-foot fronds.

D. affinis Golden-Scaled Male Fern— This species is similar to male fern but the fronds are more upright and the pinnae are layered up the frond like steps. Plants form bold 3- to 4-foot clumps in moist, humus-rich, acidic soil. Many crested selections are available. Native to Europe and Asia. Semi-evergreen, 1-pinnate pinnatifid. Zones 4 to 9.

'Crispa Gracilis'— A dwarf selection with lance-shaped fronds with curve-tipped, dull green pinnae. *(continues on the next page)*

'Cristata Angustata'— This selection has narrow 2-foot fronds with rounded, densely crested pinnae.

'Cristata' (Also ' The King')— A popular cultivar with fan-shaped, crested pinnae and frond tips.

'Revolvens'— This selection has backward-rolled pinnae.

D. cycadina Shaggy Shield Fern— This bold fern has bright green, lance-shaped fronds with simple, coarsely toothed pinnae. The stiff fronds radiate in an open vase shape from a central crown. The fiddleheads and young fronds are clothed in dense black scales. Plants grow best in moist, acidic, humus-rich soil. Native to India and Asia. Evergreen, 1-pinnate. Zones 4 to 9.

D. erythrosora Autumn Fern— Autumn fern is rapidly becoming one of the most popular garden ferns. The broad, triangular fronds emerge copper-colored in spring and unfurl to a pinkish green. Mature fronds are deep shiny green and may reach 18 inches in height. The sori, which are produced in the fall, are bright red. Plants thrive in moist, neutral to acidic, humus-rich soil in light to full shade. Native to China, Japan and Korea. Evergreen, 2-pinnate. Zones 5 to 9. Trail in zone 4.

D. marginalis Marginal Wood Fern— This tough, adaptable fern has a place in every garden. The stiff, 1- to 2-foot, arching fronds are dull olive-green in color and arise in a vase shape from a central crown. The sori are distinctive in that they are borne along the margins of the pinnules. Plants grow in moist, well drained neutral to acidic, humus-rich soil in partial to full shade. Established plants are drought tolerant. Native to eastern and central North America. Evergreen, 1-pinnate pinnatifid to 2-pinnate. Zones 4 to 8.

D. affinis, golden-scaled male fern

D. erythrosora, autumn fern, showing bright red sori

Dryopteris goldiana

Goldie's Wood Fern, Giant Wood Fern

NATIVE HABITAT: Eastern and central North America from Quebec to Ontario south to Georgia and Missouri

HARDINESS ZONES: 4 to 8

OUTSTANDING FEATURES: Goldie's fern is a giant among wood ferns. The upright, arching oval to triangular fronds arise from a stout rhizome with an elevated crown. The flattened pinnae are pale green along the margins, giving young fronds a two-tone effect. Rounded sori with kidney-shaped indusia are borne in regular rows along the midveins of the fertile pinnules. Plants grow 3 to 4 feet tall. The deciduous fronds are 1-pinnate pinnatifid.

GARDEN USE: Use goldie's ferns singly or in small groups for a tall, vertical accent. Combine them with strap-leaved plants such as iris, strongly vertical plants such as solomon's seal and plants with broad foliage such as lungworts and 'Montrose Ruby' coral bells.

HOW TO GROW: Plant goldie's ferns in moist, neutral to acidic, humus-rich soil in partial to full shade. Fronds turn pale yellow in autumn. Established plants are difficult to move.

CULTIVARS AND RELATED SPECIES

D. celsa Log Fern— This fern is similar to the above but is smaller in stature and has narrower fronds. Plants grow in wet, acidic, highly organic soils, often on rotting wood as the common name indicates. Native to the mid-Atlantic and southeastern United States west to Illinois. Deciduous, 1-pinnate pinnatifid. Zones 5 to 9.

D. ludoviciana Southern Wood Fern— This species resembles goldie's fern but the erect, stiff fronds are narrow, lance-shaped and taper at both ends. Plants grow 2 to 4 feet tall in moist to wet, acidic, humus-rich soils in sun or shade. Native to the southeastern coastal plain west to Texas. Slightly dimorphic evergreen, 1-pinnate pinnatifid. Zones 6 to 10.

Gymnocarpium dryopteris
OAK FERN

NATIVE HABITAT: Northern North America from Labrador and Alaska south to Virginia and Arizona

HARDINESS ZONE: 2 to 8

OUTSTANDING FEATURES: Oak fern is a dainty creeper that forms lacy mats of fronds that hug the forest floor. The deeply dissected, triangular three-part fronds arise in rows along the trailing rhizome. Small, rounded naked sori are borne at the ends of the veins of the pinnules. Plants grow 6 to 10 inches tall, rarely larger. The deciduous fronds are 3-pinnate.

GARDEN USE: Plant oak fern as a delicate groundcover beneath larger ferns and wildflowers such as baneberry, false solomon's seal and astilbe. Use with spring bulbs such as snowdrops under flowering shrubs.

HOW TO GROW: Plant oak fern in moist, acidic, humus-rich soil in partial to full shade. Plants are intolerant of high temperatures and dry winds. Divide overgrown clumps in fall.

CULTIVARS AND RELATED SPECIES

G. robertianum Limestone Oak Fern— This fern is similar to oak fern but has narrower, glandular blades and is weakly three-parted. Plants grow 8 to 18 inches in moist, neutral humus-rich soils . Native to the Northern portion of oak fern's range. Deciduous, 2-pinnate pinnatifid. Zones 2 to 7.

Oak fern forms lacy mats of fronds that hug the forest floor.

Matteuccia struthiopteris
OSTRICH FERN

NATIVE HABITAT: Northern North America from Newfoundland to Alaska, south to Virginia, the Great Lakes and British Columbia; Eurasia

HARDINESS: Zone 2 to 8

OUTSTANDING FEATURES: Ostrich fern is a popular garden plant throughout its range and beyond. The tall plume-shaped sterile fronds arise in a narrow vase shape from a creeping, crown-forming rhizome. They taper gradually toward the base and are widest at the top. The tip of the frond is abruptly constricted. Sori are borne on separate reduced fertile fronds with stiff pinnae. Plants grow 3 to 5 feet tall. The deciduous sterile fronds are 1-pinnate pinnatifid. The persistent fertile fronds release their spores in the spring. The fiddleheads are edible.

Fertile fronds in the winter garden

GARDEN USE: Use ostrich fern as a foundation plant or in drifts in the woodland garden. Combine them with spring flowering bulbs, wildflowers and garden perennials. The fronds emerge early and make vertical accents among groundcovers such as sweet woodruff, epimedium, foamflower and trillium.

HOW TO GROW: Plant ostrich fern in moist, neutral, humus-rich soil in light to full shade. Plants in cool, wet locations tolerate full sun. Clumps spread rapidly and may be invasive. Remove crowns that spread beyond their position. Divide plants in fall.

Onoclea sensibilis
SENSITIVE FERN

NATIVE HABITAT: Eastern and Central North America from Labrador and Manitoba, south to Florida and Colorado

HARDINESS ZONE: 2 to 10

OUTSTANDING FEATURES: Sensitive fern produces a carpet of pale sea-green sterile fronds from a fast-creeping rhizome. The fronds turn yellow to russet in the autumn and are easily killed by frost, hence the common name of sensitive fern. This highly dimorphic fern bears bead-like sori on specialized fertile fronds that persist through the winter and release their spores the following season. Plants grow 1 to 2 1/2 feet tall. The deciduous fronds are pinnatifid to 1-pinnate.

Fertile fronds with bead-like sori

GARDEN USE: Combine sensitive fern with tough perennials that thrive in moist soil such as Siberian iris, hosta, astilbe and turtlehead. The persistent fertile fronds add a nice dimension to the winter landscape and are prized for dried flower arrangements.

HOW TO GROW: Plant sensitive fern in moist to wet, neutral to acidic, humus-rich soil in sun or shade. These tough plants thrive in a variety of conditions. Their adaptability and fast growth have brought them both scorn and praise. Plants need frequent division to keep them in bounds but their exquisite fronds make them worth the trouble.

Osmunda cinnamomea
Cinnamon Fern

NATIVE HABITAT: Eastern North America from Labrador to Ontario, south to Florida and Texas

HARDINESS ZONE: 3 to 10

OUTSTANDING FEATURES: Cinnamon fern is a statuesque plant that is a valuable addition to the garden from early spring through frost. The erect clusters of emerging fiddleheads are clothed in tawny hairs. They radiate from a stout, wiry, crown-forming rhizome. From the center of the clump arise congested, deep green fertile fronds that turn bright cinnamon-brown as they mature, hence the common name. The lustrous sterile fronds form a tall arching vase that matures as the ephemeral fertile fronds wither. In autumn, the fronds turn russet to golden. Plants grow 2 to 4 feet tall. The deciduous fronds are 1-pinnate pinnatifid.

GARDEN USE: Use clumps or drifts of cinnamon fern in combination with fine textured ferns, wildflowers and shrubs. They are perfect for greening up wet areas in combination with sensitive fern. Plant them as an accent next to a tree or stump where the emerging fiddleheads show off to good advantage. All osmundas are adaptable to most perennial beds, where they are a lovely foil to colorful flowers.

HOW TO GROW: Plant cinnamon fern in consistently moist to wet, acidic, humus-rich soil in sun or shade. If soil becomes dry, plants will go dormant. Chronically dry soil will kill them. All osmundas are slow to establish but are extremely long lived. Large plants are difficult to transplant due to their huge, clump-forming rhizomes. Sow spores of all osmundas as soon as they mature.

CULTIVARS AND RELATED SPECIES

O. claytoniana Interrupted Fern, Clayton's Fern — This fern is similar in appearance to cinnamon fern but the pinnae are broader and pale green in color. The fertile fronds are distinctly different. They bear both sterile and fertile pinnae on the same frond. The congested, ephemeral fertile pinnae occur half way up the frond with sterile pinnae above and below, thus creating an "interruption" in the frond when they fall off in summer. The 1- to 5-foot fronds emerge in a spreading vase from a wiry, crown-forming rhizome.

(continues on the next page)

Plants grow in moist, neutral to acidic, average to humus-rich soil in sun or shade. They are native from Newfoundland and Manitoba, south to North Carolina and Iowa. Dimorphic, deciduous, 1-pinnate pinnatifid. Zones 3 to 8.

O. regalis Royal Fern, Flowering Fern— This distinctive fern produces a congested cluster of bead-like sori on fertile pinnae at the tip of the fronds, giving the impression of a flower cluster. The sterile pinnae are uncharacteristic and resemble leafy stems. The fronds are pale pink as they emerge in a vase-shaped cluster from a stout, wiry, crown-forming rhizome. As fronds mature the stipe turns dark and the pinnae turn deep sea-green. Plants require consistently moist to wet, acidic, humus-rich soil in sun or shade. They grow 2 to 5 feet tall. Native from Newfoundland and Saskatchewan, south to Florida and Texas. Dimorphic, deciduous, distinctively 2-pinnate. Zones 3 to 10.

var. *regalis* 'Purpurascens'— This European variety has purple new growth, very dark stipes and large, plume-like fertile pinnae.

O. regalis 'Crispa', crisped royal fern, has wavy pinnules.

O. claytoniana showing "interrupted" frond with sterile and fertile pinnae

Pentagramma triangularis (*Pityrogramma triangularis*)

Goldback Fern

NATIVE HABITAT: Western North America from British Columbia south to Nevada, New Mexico and California

HARDINESS ZONE: 7 to 10

OUTSTANDING FEATURES: Goldback fern forms an attractive groundcover of dark green, triangular to pentagonal fronds held on tall black stipes above the creeping rhizomes. Elongated, nearly marginal sori are hidden by yellow powder on the fertile fronds, hence the common name. Plants grow 6 to 18 inches tall. The deciduous fronds are 2-pinnate pinnatifid.

GARDEN USE: Use goldback fern as a groundcover under shrubs or as an accent in rock gardens. Plants grow well in crevices in rock walls or stairs.

HOW TO GROW: Plant goldback fern in moist, acidic, humus-rich soil in light to partial shade, Established plants are extremely drought tolerant. The fronds curl up when the plants get dry, exposing the yellow undersides.

Goldback fern is extremely drought tolerant.

Phegopteris hexagonoptera
(Thelypteris hexagonoptera)

SOUTHERN BEECH FERN, BROAD BEECH FERN

NATIVE HABITAT: Eastern North America from Quebec and Ontario, south to Florida and Texas

HARDINESS ZONE: 4 to 9

OUTSTANDING FEATURES: Southern beech fern has broad, triangular fronds held horizontally on thin stipes. The fronds are produced in rows or in loose clusters along creeping rhizomes. The fronds turn pale yellow in the autumn. Round, naked sori are borne irregularly on the fertile fronds. Plants grow 1-1/2 to 2 feet tall. The deciduous fronds are 1-pinnate pinnatifid to 2-pinnate.

GARDEN USE: Use southern beech fern as an open groundcover under shrubs and small flowering trees. Combine them with upright evergreen woodferns and holly ferns or plant them with tall wildflowers such as baneberries and black cohosh.

HOW TO GROW:
Plant southern beech fern in moist, neutral to acidic, humus-rich soil in shade. In fertile garden soils plants grow rapidly and need dividing to control their spread.

CULTIVARS AND RELATED SPECIES

Phegopteris connectilis (Thelypteris phegopteris) Northern Beech Fern, Narrow Beech Fern—This fetching fern is similar to the above species but the 1 to 2-foot fronds are narrow and long. The basal pinnae are reflexed like rabbit ears so the fronds appear arrow shaped. Plants grow in moist, acidic, humus-rich soil in shade. They do not thrive where summer nights are hot. Protect plants from hot, dry winds. Native to northern North America from Labrador and Alaska, south to the mountains of North Carolina, Minnesota and Washington. Deciduous, 1-pinnate pinnatifid to 2-pinnate. Zones 3 to 8.

P. connectilis

Polypodium virginianum
Rock Fern,
Rock Polypody

NATIVE HABITAT: Newfoundland to Manitoba, south to Georgia and Arkansas

HARDINESS ZONE: 2 to 8.

OUTSTANDING FEATURES: Rock fern forms an attractive, evergreen carpet atop boulders and in rock crevices. The leathery, deep, olive-green fronds arise from a wandering rhizome that grows on the surface of the soil. The circular, naked sori are bright orange and are borne in rows along either side of the midveins of the lobes. Plants grow 8 to 10 inches tall. The evergreen fronds are deeply pinnatifid.

GARDEN USE: Use rock fern in unmortared walls, along steps or in rock gardens. They will also grow in soil along the roots of trees or in stony areas with columbines, rue anemone and bluebells.

HOW TO GROW: Plant rock fern in moist, neutral to acidic, humus-rich soil in partial to full shade. They need excellent drainage and are easiest to grow when associated with rocks. Plants will also grow in light humusy soil with stones added to insure good aeration and drainage. Established plants are extremely drought tolerant.

CULTIVARS AND RELATED SPECIES

P. glycyrrhiza Licorice Fern— Similar to rock fern but with pointed, tapering lobes. The rhizome has a sweet taste. Culture is the same as above. Plants are native from Alaska south to California. Evergreen, deeply pinnatifid. Zones 7 to 10.

P. scouleri Leathery Fern— This fern is similar to the above species but has larger fronds with few broad, blunt lobes. Plants grow on trees as well as rocks. Native from British Columbia south to California. Evergreen, deeply pinnatifid. Zones 7 to 10.

P. vulgare Common Polypody— The European counterpart to rock fern and similar in all respects. Widely grown in gardens. Evergreen, deeply pinnatifid. Zones 4 to 8.

'Bifidum'— This selection has notched lobes.

'Cristatum'— A cultivar with crested lobes and tips.

P. cambricum Southern Polypody — This lovely groundcover fern resembles common polypody but has wider fronds that taper abruptly at the tip. Plants grow on rocks and tree trunks or in loose, humus-rich soil. Native to Europe. Deciduous, deeply pinnatifid. Zones 5-10.

Polystichum acrostichoides
Christmas Fern

NATIVE HABITAT: From Nova Scotia and Ontario, south to Florida and Texas

HARDINESS ZONE: 3 to 9

OUTSTANDING FEATURES: Christmas fern produces tufted clumps of stiff, deep green, dimorphic fronds from a creeping, crown-forming rhizome. Sori covered with circular indusia are crowded on reduced pinnae on the upper 1/3 of the fertile fronds. The sterile fronds are smaller and less erect. All polystichums have scaly rhizomes and stipes. Plants grow 1 to 3 feet tall. The evergreen fronds are 1-pinnate.

GARDEN USE: Combine with other ferns in foundation plantings, along walks and steps or in woodland gardens with bulbs, wildflowers and groundcovers. The stiff fronds remain erect until hard frost or heavy snow push them over.

HOW TO GROW: Prefers moist, well-drained, neutral to acidic, humus-rich soil in light to full shade. Plants tolerate dense shade and dry soil; if soil is moist they tolerate considerable sun. Divide dense clumps in spring or fall.

CULTIVARS AND RELATED SPECIES

P. braunii Braun's Holly Fern— Forms wide, arching vases of glossy, 2 to 2 1/2-foot, deep green fronds from a creeping, crown-forming rhizome. Plants require moist, acidic, humus-rich soil in partial to full shade. Established plants tolerate dry soil. Native to Northern North America from Nova Scotia and Ontario, south to New England and Minnesota. Disjunct in Alaska and British Columbia. Semi-evergreen to deciduous, 2-pinnate. Zones 3 to 8.

P. munitum Western Sword Fern— Resembles Christmas fern but is much larger. The 3 to 5-foot fronds are slightly dimorphic, with the fertile fronds standing more erect. Plants require moist, acidic, humus-rich soil in partial to full shade. Established plants are drought tolerant. Native to western North America east to the Rocky Mountains. Evergreen, 1-pinnate. Zones 5 to 9.

P. polyblepharum Tassel Fern— A robust fern that forms an arching vase of stiff, glossy fronds from a creeping, crown-forming rhizome. The pinnae are sharply toothed and appear spiny. Plants grow 2 to 4 feet tall and are equally wide. They require moist, acidic, humus-rich soil in partial to full shade. Native to Japan, Korea and China. Slightly dimorphic, evergreen, 1 to 2-pinnate. Zones 5 to 9.

Polystichum setiferum
Soft Shield Fern

NATIVE HABITAT: Throughout Europe

HARDINESS ZONE: 5 to 9

OUTSTANDING FEATURES: Soft shield fern produces delicate billowing clumps of deeply cut, frilly fronds. Many forms have been selected for variations in the dissection of the fronds. The fronds arise in a flattened vase shape from the rhizome in the manner typical of the genus. Rust-colored sori with rounded indusia are borne near the edge of the fertile pinnae. Some forms produce plantlets along the stem that become new plants. Plants grow 2 to 4-1/2 feet tall. The evergreen fronds are 2-pinnate.

GARDEN USE: Soft shield fern is an elegant fern for use throughout the garden. Combine them with perennials in formal and informal gardens, use them as a groundcover under shrubs or plant them to soften walls and foundations.

HOW TO GROW: Plant soft shield ferns in moist, neutral to mildly acidic, humus-rich soil in light to full shade. Divide the branching rhizomes in spring or fall. Propagate by removing the plantlets as they begin to form fronds.

CULTIVARS AND RELATED SPECIES

'Congestum Cristatum'— A dwarf selection with constricted pinnule segments.

'Divisilobum'— This frilly selection has 3 to 4-pinnate fronds with finely divided segments.

'Rotundatum Cristatum'— Upright selection with rounded pinnae and crested frond tips.

P. aculeatum Hard Shield Fern— Similar to soft shield fern but its stiff, glossy fronds are more upright and the pinnae are more congested along the rachis. Grows 2 to 3 feet tall. Best planted in moist, neutral, humus-rich soils in partial to full shade. Native to Europe and Asia. Evergreen, 1-pinnate pinnatifid to 2-pinnate. Zones 6 to 9.

P. andersonii Anderson's Holly Fern— Resembles hard shield fern but has taller fronds with longer pinnae. Plantlets are produced near the tip of the 2 to 3-1/2 -foot fronds. Plants grow in moist, acidic, humus-rich soil in partial to full shade. Native from Alaska to Montana. Evergreen, 1-pinnate pinnatifid to 2-pinnate. Zones 6 to 9.

P. tsus-simense Korean Rock Fern— This diminutive member of the genus bears 12-inch, triangular to lance-shaped, deep green fronds from a creeping, crown-forming rhizome. Give plants moist, neutral, humus-rich soil in partial to full shade. They are often grown as house plants. Native to China, Japan and Korea. Evergreen, 2-pinnate. Zones 6 to 9.

Sphaeropteris cooperi (*Cyathea cooperi*)

LACY TREE FERN

NATIVE HABITAT: Australia

HARDINESS ZONE: 9 to 11

OUTSTANDING FEATURES: This popular tree fern has huge, lacy, pale-green fronds radiating from a central crown atop a slender trunk. Each 10-foot frond is supported by a stout stipe and rachis. Rounded, indusiate sori are scattered on the pinnules of the fertile fronds. Plants grow 8 to 16 feet tall. The evergreen fronds are 3-pinnate.

GARDEN USE: Lacy tree ferns are popular as accents in sub-tropical gardens. They lend an exotic flavor to courtyards, entryways and large gardens. Combine them with flowering and evergreen shrubs and other ferns. They also grow well in containers.

HOW TO GROW: Plant lacy tree fern in constantly moist, well drained, humus-rich soil in full to partial sun. They require lots of fertilizer and respond well to an annual top-dressing with composted manure. Protect plants from strong winds, which may desiccate the fronds or topple the plants.

A look down at the canopy of lacy tree fern

Thelypteris kunthii
Southern Maiden Fern,
River Fern

NATIVE HABITAT: Southeastern United States from South Carolina to Texas and Arkansas

HARDINESS ZONE: 7 to 10

OUTSTANDING FEATURES: Southern maiden fern forms a beautiful tangle of bright sea-green fronds from a long-creeping, branching rhizome. The sori with rounded indusia are borne along the midveins of the pinna lobes. Plants grow 2 to 4 feet tall, occasionally larger. The deciduous fronds are 1-pinnate pinnatifid.

GARDEN USE: Use southern maiden fern in mass plantings with shrubs or in combination with large perennials such as joe-pye weed, New England aster and iris. In the shaded garden plant them with hostas, ligularias, ornamental rhubarbs and grasses.

HOW TO GROW: Plant southern maiden fern in moist to wet, acidic, average to humus-rich soil in sun or shade. Plants are fast growing and may become weedy, especially in moist fertile soil. Divide overgrown clumps in spring or fall.

CULTIVARS AND RELATED SPECIES

Macrothelypteris torresiana (*Thelypteris torresiana*) Mariana Maiden Fern — A tall fern that produces deeply dissected, lanceolate fronds from a creeping rhizome. Plants require moist to wet, neutral to acidic, humus-rich soil in partial to full shade. Native to Asia, Australia, Africa and Malaysia. Also found in a few scattered localities in the Southeast, perhaps as an escape from cultivation. Deciduous, 2-pinnate, bipinnatifid. Zones 8 to 11.

Thelypteris noveboracensis New York Fern — Produces tight mats of upright, 1 to 2-foot, bright green fronds from fast-creeping rhizomes. Fronds turn golden yellow to straw-colored in autumn. Plants require moist, neutral to moderately acidic, humus-rich soil in sun or shade. Native to Eastern North America from Newfoundland and Ontario, south to Georgia and Mississippi. Deciduous, 1-pinnate pinnatifid. Zones 3 to 8.

T. palustris Marsh Fern — This species produces wiry, bright green fronds in a line or loose clump from a fast-creeping rhizome. The narrow 2 to 3-1/2-foot fronds have shiny black stipes. Plants grow in moist to wet, neutral to acidic, humus-rich soil in sun or shade. They even grow in shallow water. Native to Eastern and Central North America from Newfoundland and Manitoba, south to Florida, South Dakota and Texas. Slightly dimorphic, deciduous, 1-pinnate pinnatifid. Zones 2 to 9.

Woodsia obtusa

BLUNT-LOBED WOODSIA,

CLIFF FERN

NATIVE HABITAT: Eastern and Central North America from Maine and Quebec, south to Georgia, Nebraska and Texas

HARDINESS ZONE: 4 to 9

OUTSTANDING FEATURES: Blunt-lobed woodsia is an easy-to-grow rock fern with lacy, deep-green fronds from a slow-creeping rhizome. Rounded sori surrounded by ragged indusia are borne at the tips of the veins of the pinnules. Plants grow 1 to 1 1/2 feet tall. The deciduous fronds are 2-pinnate. Several additional species of *Woodsia* are grown.

GARDEN USE: Use blunt-lobed woodsia in rock gardens, in walls and along steps to soften lines. Combine them with other rock-loving plants such as columbines, rue anemones and sedums.

HOW TO GROW: Plant blunt-lobed woodsia in moist but well-drained, neutral to moderately acidic humus-rich soil in rock crevices or among stones. Good drainage is essential. Plants may be short-lived in cultivation.

CULTIVARS AND RELATED SPECIES

W. ilvensis Rusty Woodsia — A diminutive rock fern, rusty woodsia gets its name from the tawny brown scales on the undersides of the pinnae. Plants grow 3 to 6 inches tall from dense, tufted crowns. The plant requires slightly acidic, well drained, airy soil in full to partial sun. Native to northern North America south to Pennsylvania, Iowa and British Columbia and the mountains of North Carolina. Deciduous. 1-pinnate pinnatifid to 2-pinnate. Zones 1 to 6.

W. polystichoides — This attractive fern produces erect, 6- to 8-inch clumps of narrow, silvery fronds from a congested crown. Plants grow in acidic, humus-rich soil among rocks in light to partial shade. Native to China, Japan and Korea. Deciduous. 1-pinnate. Zones 5 to 8.

W. scopulina Rocky Mountain Woodsia — A rock fern that produces dense clumps of erect, 3- to 4-inch, soft, hairy fronds from a tight crown. Plants grow in well drained, acid humus among rocks and rock crevices. Native to northern North America south to northern Mexico, the Great Lakes and Nova Scotia. Deciduous. 2-pinnate to 2-pinnate pinnatifid. Zones 2 to 9.

Woodwardia areolata

NETTED CHAIN FERN

NATIVE HABITAT: Coastal areas of Eastern North America from Nova Scotia to Texas

HARDINESS ZONE: 5 to 9

OUTSTANDING FEATURES: Netted chain fern has bright green fronds that grow in lines or loose clusters along creeping rhizomes. The sterile fronds resemble sensitive fern with flat wide pinnae at the base and narrower lobes toward the top of the fronds. Elongated sori with thin indusia are borne in chain-like formations on the linear segments of the fertile fronds. Plants grow 1 to 2 feet tall. Dimorphic, deciduous, 1-pinnate below to pinnatifid above.

GARDEN USE: Combine netted chain fern with wet-soil plants such as iris, astilbe, drooping sedge and rodgersia. They grow well in bog gardens but also tolerate moist garden soil. Do not allow plants to dry out.

HOW TO GROW: Plant netted chain fern in constantly moist to wet, acidic, humus-rich soil in light to full shade. Divide plants in spring or fall if they overgrow their position.

CULTIVARS AND RELATED SPECIES

W. fimbriata Giant Chain Fern — This fern produces huge oval to broadly lance-shaped fronds from a stout creeping rhizome. The coarse, evergreen fronds have deeply cut, ragged pinnae with pointed lobes. Plants grow up to 6 or more feet tall. Elongated indusiate sori are born in chain-like formations on the fertile fronds. Plants grow in moist to wet, acidic, sandy to humus-rich soil in sun or shade. Native to the west coast from British Columbia to California. Evergreen, 1-pinnate pinnatifid. Zones 7 to 9.

W. virginica Virginia Chain Fern — A smaller version of giant chain fern with rounded pinna lobes. The 3 to 4-foot fronds are deep green and lustrous with black stipes. Plants grow in moist to wet, acidic, sandy to humus-rich soil in sun or shade. Native to eastern North America from New Brunswick and Quebec, south to Florida and Arkansas. Deciduous, 1-pinnate pinnatifid. Zones 4 to 10.

TOP TEN FERNS BY REGION

The following are some of the best all-around performers in typical garden situations. They're also widely available, attractive, adaptable and durable when planted in the proper site. Consult the Encyclopedia for appropriate growing conditions.

NORTHEAST

Adiantum pedatum
Maidenhair fern
Athyrium filix-femina
Lady Fern

Thelypteris noveboracensis

Dryopteris filix-mas
Male Fern
Dryopteris goldiana
Goldie's Fern
Gymnocarpium dryopteris
Oak Fern
Matteuccia struthiopteris
Ostrich Fern
Osmunda cinnamomea
Cinnamon Fern
Phegopteris connectilis
Northern Beech Fern
Polystichum acrostichoides
Christmas Fern
Thelypteris noveboracensis
New York Fern

SOUTHEAST

Athyrium filix-femina
Lady Fern
Dryopteris erythrosora
Autumn Fern
Dryopteris ludoviciana
Southern Wood Fern
Osmunda cinnamomea
Cinnamon Fern
Osmunda regalis
Royal Fern
Phegopteris hexagonoptera
Southern Beech Fern
Polypodium virginianum
Rock Fern
Polystichum acrostichoides
Christmas Fern

Dryopteris ludoviciana

Thelypteris kunthii
River Fern
Woodwardia areolata
Netted Chain Fern

SOUTHERN GREAT PLAINS/ TEXAS

Adiantum capillus-veneris

Adiantum capillus-veneris
Southern Maidenhair Fern
Cyrtomium falcatum
Holly Fern
Dryopteris erythrosora
Autumn Fern
Dryopteris ludoviciana
Southern Wood Fern
Onoclea sensibilis
Sensitive Fern
Osmunda regalis
Royal Fern
Polystichum acrostichoides

Christmas Fern
Polystichum polyblepharum
Tassel Fern
Polystichum tsus-simense
Korean Rock Fern
Thelypteris kunthii
River Fern

NORTHERN GREAT PLAINS/ GREAT LAKES

Adiantum pedatum
Maidenhair Fern
Athyrium filix-femina
Lady Fern
Athyrium niponicum
'Pictum' Japanese Painted Fern
Diplazium pycnocarpon
Glade Fern
Dryopteris filix-mas
Male Fern

Dryopteris marginalis

Dryopteris marginalis
Marginal Wood Fern
Matteuccia struthiopteris
Ostrich Fern
Osmunda claytoniana
Interrupted Fern
Phegopteris connectilis
Northern Beech Fern
Polystichum acrostichoides
Christmas Fern

ROCKY MOUNTAINS/ GREAT BASIN

Adiantum pedatum
Maidenhair Fern
Asplenium trichomanes
Maidenhair Spleenwort

Polystichum andersonii

Athyrium filix-femina var. *cyclosorum*
Western Lady Fern
Athyrium niponicum
'Pictum' Japanese Painted Fern
Cystopteris fragilis
Fragile Fern
Dryopteris filix-mas
Male Fern
Dryopteris marginalis
Marginal Wood Fern
Matteuccia struthiopteris
Ostrich Fern
Polystichum aculeatum
Hard Shield Fern
Polystichum andersonii
Anderson's Holly Fern

PACIFIC NORTHWEST

Adiantum aleuticum
Western Maidenhair Fern
Blechnum penna-marina
Little Hard Fern
Blechnum spicant
Deer Fern
Dryopteris affinis
Golden-Scaled Male Fern
Dryopteris dilatata
Broad Wood Fern
Dryopteris erythrosora
Autumn Fern
Osmunda regalis
Royal Fern
Polystichum munitum
Western Sword Fern
Polystichum polyblepharum
Tassel Fern
Polystichum setiferum
Soft Shield Fern

Blechnum penna-marina

CALIFORNIA/ COASTAL AREAS

Adiantum pedatum
Maidenhair Fern

Athyrium filix-femina
Lady Fern
Blechnum spicant
Deer Fern

Polystichum polyblepharum

Dryopteris dilatata
Broad Wood Fern
Dryopteris erythrosora
Autumn Fern
Pentagramma triangularis
Goldback Fern
Polypodium scouleri
Leathery Fern
Polystichum munitum
Western Sword Fern
Polystichum polyblepharum
Tassel Fern
Woodwardia fimbriata
Giant Chain Fern

SUBTROPICAL FLORIDA

Blechnum serrulatum
Swamp Water Fern
Cyrtomium falcatum
Holly Fern
Dennstaedtia bipinnata
Cuplet Fern
Dicksonia antarctica
Soft Tree Fern
Dryopteris erythrosora
Autumn Fern
Macrothelypteris torresiana
Mariana Maiden Fern
Osmunda cinnamomea
Cinnamon Fern
Osmunda regalis
Royal Fern
Sphaeropteris cooperi
Lacy Tree Fern
Thelypteris kunthii
Southern Maiden Fern

NEW & UNUSUAL FERNS

Adiantum venustum
Evergreen Maidenhair
Arachniodes standishii
Upside-down Fern
Blechnum cordatum
Dryopteris bissetiana
Dryopteris crassirhizoma
Dryopteris formosana
Dryopteris lepidopoda

Dryopteris sublacera

Dryopteris sublacera
Marsilea macropoda
Water Fern
Microlepia strigosa
Lace Fern
Polystichum makinoi
Polystichum neolobatum
Woodsia polystichoides

ROCK FERNS FOR THE SPECIALIST

Asplenium ruta-muraria
Wall Rue
Asplenium viride
Green Spleenwort
Ceterach officinarum
Rusty-back Fern
Cheilanthes lanosa
Hairy Lip Fern

Ceterach officinarum

Cheilanthes feei
Slender Lip Fern
Cryptogramma acrostichoides
Parsley Fern
Pellaea andromedifolia
Coffee Fern
Pellaea atropurpurea
Purple Cliff Brake
Pellaea ternifolia
Ternate Cliff Break
Woodsia ilvensis
Rusty Woodsia
Woodsia scopulina
Rocky Mountain Woodsia

WHERE TO SEE FERNS

BY CHARLOTTE A. JONES-ROE

One of the best ways to learn how to recognize and grow ferns is to visit gardens in which they are displayed in collections or used in the landscape. Collections that feature many different ferns enable you to do side-by-side comparison and are a great aid in learning to recognize the different types of ferns. Landscape plantings demonstrate the form, growth habit and cultural requirements of ferns hardy in the area.

The following list is not exhaustive; many other public gardens feature ferns in the landscape or in collections. Most of the gardens profiled below are listed as featuring ferns in the *Plant Collections Directory* of the American Association of Botanic Gardens and Arboreta. Call for details on opening hours and featured ferns.

The Botanic Garden of Smith College, Northampton, MA 01063; (413) 585-2748

Institute of Ecosystem Studies, The Mary Flagler Cary Arboretum, Box AB, Millbrook, NY 12545; (914) 677-5358

Brooklyn Botanic Garden, 1000 Washington Ave., Brooklyn, NY 11225; (718) 622-4433

The New York Botanical Garden, Southern Blvd., Bronx, NY 10458; (718) 817-8705

Tupper Hill/Norcross Wildlife Sanctuary, 30 Peck Rd., Monson, MA 01057; (413) 267-9654.

Bowman's Hill Wildflower Preserve, Box 103, River Rd., Rte. 32, Washington Crossing, PA 18977; (215) 862-2924

The Marie Selby Botanical Gardens, 811 South Palm Ave., Sarasota, FL 33577; (813) 366-5731

Birmingham Botanical Gardens, 2612 Lane Park Rd., Birmingham, AL 35223; (205) 879-1227

Fernwood Botanic Gardens, 13988 Range Line Rd., Niles, MI 49120; (616) 695-6491

University of California Botanical Garden at Berkeley, Centennial Dr., Berkeley, CA 94720; (510) 643-8040.

U.S. National Arboretum, 3501 New York Avenue, NE, Washington, DC 20002; (202) 475-4815

Rhododendron Species Foundation, Box 3798, Federal Way, WA 98063-3798; (206) 661-9377

North Carolina Botanical Garden, Totten Center CB# 3375, University of North Carolina, Chapel Hill, NC 27599-3375; (919) 962-0522

Morris Arboretum of the University of Pennsylvania, Dorrance H. Hamilton Fernery, 9414 Meadowbrook Ave., Philadelphia, PA 19118; (215) 247-5777

(continues on the next page)

DENVER BOTANIC GARDENS, 909 York Street, Denver, CO 80206; (303) 331-4000

MATTHAEI BOTANICAL GARDENS, University of Michigan, 1800 North Dixboro Rd., Ann Arbor, MI 48105; (313) 998-7061

WAIMEA ARBORETUM AND BOTANICAL GARDENS, 59-864 Kamehameha Hwy, Haleiwa, Oahu, HI 96712; (808) 638-8655

GARDEN IN THE WOODS, New England Wild Flower Society, Hemenway Rd., Framingham, MA 01701; (508) 877-7630

WHERE TO GET FERNS

FANCY FRONDS (affiliate of **BARFOD'S HARDY FERNS**) 1911 Fourth Ave. West, Seattle, WA 98119; (206) 284-5332. Catalog, $1

FOLIAGE GARDENS, 2003 128th Ave., SE, Bellevue, WA 98005; (206) 747-2998. Catalog, $2

KURT BLUEMEL, INC., 2740 Greene La., Baldwin, MD 21013-9523; (410) 557-7229. Catalog $3

RAINFOREST GARDENS, 13139 224th St., RR2, Maple Ridge, BC V2X 7E7 Canada; (604) 467-4218. Catalog, $2

SISKIYOU RARE PLANT NURSERY, 2825 Cummings Rd., Medford, OR 97501; (503) 772-6846. Catalog, $2

SUNLIGHT GARDENS, 174 Golden Lane, Andersonville, TN 37705; (615) 494-8237. Catalog, $3

WE-DU NURSERIES, Rte. 5, Box 724, Marion, NC 28752; (704) 738-8300. Catalog, $2

FERN SOCIETIES

Fern societies offer publications, plants and spores. Officers and contacts may change from year to year.

AMERICAN FERN SOCIETY, Dr. Richard L. Hauke, 456 McGill Pl., Atlanta, GA 30312

BIRMINGHAM FERN SOCIETY, Birmingham Botanical Gardens, 2612 Park Rd. Birmingham, AL 35223

CORPUS CHRISTI FERN SOCIETY, c/o P. Coleman, 438 Claremont St., Corpus Christi, TX 78412

DELAWARE VALLEY FERN & WILDFLOWER SOCIETY, c/o Mrs. Alice Blake Simonson, 1030 Limekin Pike, Maple Glen, PA 19002

HARDY FERN FOUNDATION, Box 166, Medina, WA 98039-0166

HARDY PLANT SOCIETY, Mid Atlantic Group c/o Joanne Walkovic 539 Woodland Avenue Media, PA 19063

HARDY PLANT SOCIETY OF OREGON, Box 609 Beaverton, OR 97005

LOS ANGELES INTERNATIONAL FERN SOCIETY, Box 90943, Pasadena, CA 91109-0943

LOUISIANA FERN SOCIETY, c/o Mary Elliott 8335 Birch St.,

PHOTO CREDITS

Cover and inside photos by C. Colston Burrell, except:
pages 1, 22-25, 60, 82, 90, 102 1st & 2nd col.: Judith Jones;
page 101 1st col.: Galen Gates;
page 31: Roger L. Hammer
pages 6-7, 39, 42, 44, 61: Jerry Pavia;
pages 10, 37: Joanne Pavia;
pages 40, 92, 93: Pamela Harper;
pages 47, 68, 80, 83, 88, 96, 101 2nd & 3rd col., 102 3rd col.: Sue Olsen;
page 69, 81: Stephen K-M. Tim

New Orleans, LA 70118

Memphis Fern Society, c/o Ms. B. Feuerstein, 2357 Thornwood La., Memphis, TN 38138

Southwestern Fern Society, c/o Ms. Debbie DeBruin, 515 S. Lois La., Richardson, TX 75081

West Florida Fern Society, c/o Dr. M. Cousen, Dept. of Biology, University of West Florida, Pensacola, FL 32504

GLOSSARY

Agar an easily sterilized gelatinous substance derived from seaweed to which nutrients are often added to support the growth of certain microorganisms

Annulus the ring of thick-walled elastic cells that partially or wholly surround, and ultimately open, the spore cases

Antheridium (plural: antheridia) the male organ on the prothallus bearing the sperm cells

Archegonium (plural: archegonia) the female egg-producing organ on the prothallus

Blade the portion of a frond bearing the foliage but not including the stipe

Chaff sporangial debris, hairs and scales found mixed with spores

Crown the tip of the stem (or rhizome)

Crozier young coiled frond; fiddlehead

Dehisce burst open spontaneously to release spores

Dimorphic having two different forms, as in fronds, one usually sterile, the other fertile

False indusium a flap of blade margin folded over to cover sporangia

Fertile fronds fronds bearing spore-producing organs

Fiddleheads SEE CROZIER

Frond a fern leaf,

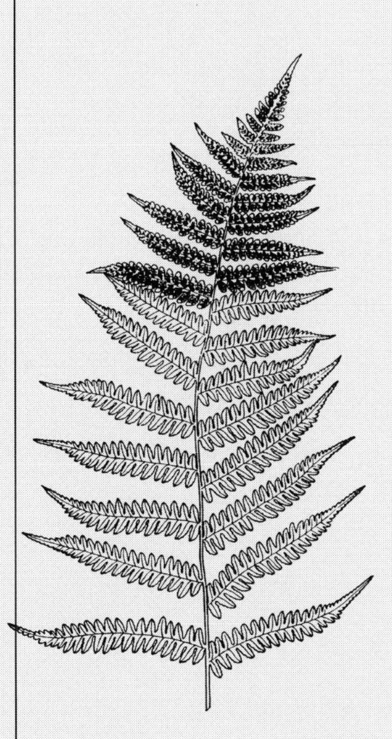

including the stipe and blade

Gametophyte the prothallus, which bears the sexual organs

Hybridization crossing two genetically different parents to make a new plant

Indument covering of hairs and scales

Indusium (plural: indusia) the membrane covering the sorus

Lamina SEE BLADE

Medium (plural: media) substance supporting the growth of plants or microorganisms

Meiosis cell division, usually in spore formation, in which the number of chromosomes of the daughter cells is reduced to half that of the parent cell

Mitosis nuclear division in which the nucleus divides into two cells, each with exactly the same number of chromosomes and genetic make-up as that of the parent nucleus

Nucleus cellular body (in cells with a nucleus) containing the genetic information necessary for such functions as growth and reproduction

Pinna (plural: pinnae) primary division of a compound fern frond

Pinna rachis the midvein of a pinna that comes off the major rachis of the frond. Also costa

Pinnate fern frond that is once divided with the divisions extending to the rachis. Pinnae so formed are arranged along either side of the rachis. Bipinnate is twice pinnate, i.e., with the pinnae bearing pinnules.

Pinnatifid fern frond that is once divided with the divisions not extending to the rachis. Bipinnatifid is twice pinnatifid.

Pinnule a secondary division of a fern frond

Proliferous bearing buds or bulbils on the fronds

Prothallus (plural: prothalli) the free-living fern generation developing from the germination of a spore and containing the sexual organs necessary to produce a new plant

Rachis the main stalk or axis of a compound fern frond

Rhizoids the rootlike structures put down by the prothallus for attachment and absorption

Rhizome a horizontally, sometimes erect growing stem from which fronds and roots arise

Simple refers to a fern blade that is not divided in any way

Sorus (plural: sori) a cluster of sporangia arranged in a distinctive pattern in each fern genus

Sporangium (plural: sporangia) a spore case in which spores develop

Spore a unicellular reproductive unit of ferns. These arise in the sporangia of the sporophytic plant and germinate to form the gametophyte

Sporophyte the conspicuous spore-bearing generation of a fern

Sterile fronds fronds that do not bear spore-producing organs

Stipe leaf stalk of fern; the portion below the blade

Zygote cell formed by the union of two gametes; gives rise to the sporophyte

HARDINESS ZONE MAP

USDA Plant Hardiness Zone Map

AVERAGE ANNUAL MINIMUM TEMPERATURE

Temperature (°C)	Zone	Temperature (°F)
-45.6 and Below	1	Below -50
-42.8 to -45.5	2a	-45 to -50
-40.0 to -42.7	2b	-40 to -45
-37.3 to -40.0	3a	-35 to -40
-34.5 to -37.2	3b	-30 to -35
-31.7 to -34.4	4a	-25 to -30
-28.9 to -31.6	4b	-20 to -25
-26.2 to -28.8	5a	-15 to -20
-23.4 to -26.1	5b	-10 to -15
-20.6 to -23.3	6a	-5 to -10
-17.8 to -20.5	6b	0 to -5
-15.0 to -17.7	7a	5 to 0
-12.3 to -15.0	7b	10 to 5
-9.5 to -12.2	8a	15 to 10
-6.7 to -9.4	8b	20 to 15
-3.9 to -6.6	9a	25 to 20
-1.2 to -3.8	9b	30 to 25
1.6 to -1.1	10a	35 to 30
4.4 to 1.7	10b	40 to 35
4.5 and Above	11	40 and Above

INDEX